BIRDS
OF THE WORLD
IN COLOR

by the same author

MAMMALS OF THE WORLD
FISHES OF THE WORLD
REPTILES AND AMPHIBIANS OF THE WORLD

BIRDS
OF THE WORLD

by Hans Hvass

Translated by
GWYNNE VEVERS

Illustrated by
WILHELM EIGENER

METHUEN & C° LTD
11 NEW FETTER LANE
LONDON E C 4

First published by
Politikens Forlag in 1961
as Alverdens Fugle

Copyright in all countries
signatory to the Berne Convention

English Translation first published 1963
Reprinted 1963, 1965 and 1968
© *1963 by Methuen & Co Ltd*

Printed in Belgium by
Casterman S. A.

SBN 416 25980   4/01
Edition 1.4

Contents

Foreword

THIS BOOK deals with the birds of the world, but not with all the birds of the world—such a book does not exist. Special attention has been given to those birds which one can expect to find in a popular zoological book, not only the common ones but also the rarities amongst the existing 8,000 to 9,000 bird species; a number of the birds described are, indeed, not actual species, but geographical races or subspecies. Practically all the European birds are illustrated and discussed, and emphasis has also been placed on the bird world of North America. For tropical birds all the characteristic species are represented, and in cases where a family is spread over most of the earth we have described and illustrated one or two species from each of the different regions where the family is found. If a family is rich in species the most interesting have been chosen, and in the case of a very popular group, such as the parrots or the birds of paradise, a large number of species has been dealt with.

In the text little is said about the appearance of the birds as this is apparent from the paintings, but special attention has been given to the distribution or range of each species.

The illustrations have been specially drawn for this book and the selection of species has been done in collaboration with the artist Wilhelm Eigener.

The birds belong among the Vertebrates, which are divided into six classes; mammals, birds, reptiles, amphibians, bony fish, selachians or cartilaginous fish, such as dogfish and sharks, and the cyclostomes which include the lampreys and hagfish. The mammals and the birds are warm-blooded, that is their body temperature remains constant and independent of their surroundings, while all the others are cold-blooded. The body temperature of birds is a few degrees higher than that of mammals.

The birds may be briefly characterised as animals clad in feathers, a definition which immediately separates them from all other living beings. In addition they are warm-blooded, breathe with lungs, have a four-chambered heart and lay

7

eggs; the beak is horn-clad and lacks teeth, the forelimbs are developed into wings, which are sometimes reduced and useless for flight, and the back limbs are mostly used for walking, running or swimming.

In this book the different groups of birds have been arranged or classified with the more advanced or highly developed species at the beginning. It should, however, be noted that many authorities nowadays use a classification that starts with the more primitive birds, such as ostriches and kiwis, and ends with the perching birds or passerines. The technical arguments on the best type of classification need not concern us here, where our primary interest is to show the enormous range of form, colour and habitat of the living birds of the world.

The birds illustrated in this book are given an English name followed by a scientific or Latin name, which is printed in italics. These names are followed by a figure which gives the body length from the tip of the bill to the tip of the tail; if there are two figures it usually means that there is a size difference between the two sexes.

The following books will be of interest to those who wish to extend their knowledge of the birds of the world :
Darling, Louis and Lois. *Bird*. Houghton, 1962.
Fisher, James. *A History of Birds*. Hillary, 1954.
Gilliard, E.T. *Living Birds of the World*. Doubleday, 1958.
Heinroth, O. and K. *The Birds*. Ann Arbor Books, 1958.
Peterson, R.T., Mountfort, Guy and Hollom, P.A.D. *A Field Guide to the Birds of Britain and Europe*. Houghton, 1954.
Peterson, R.T. *How to Know the Birds*. Houghton, 1962.
Peterson, R.T. *Field Guide to the Birds*. *Rev. Ed.* Houghton, 1959.

Passerines

THE PASSERINES, Passeriformes, consist of over 5,000 species, far more than all the other bird orders put together. Most passerines are small or medium-sized birds and they are found widely distributed over the whole of the earth except in the Antarctic; the greatest number of species is found in the tropics. The majority of them live in woods or at any rate where there are trees and bushes. They always have four toes, of which the first is directed backwards, is the most powerfully developed and has the longest claw.

There is not complete agreement on the subdivisions within the passerine group order, but here they are divided into some 56 families.

Troupials

The troupials, Icteridae, consist of nearly 100 species of sparrow- to crow-sized birds, and are found in America, mostly in the tropical regions. They are sociable, lively birds, which go about in flocks, and a number of them are quite good singers. The food varies and may consist of insects, larvae, fruit and seeds. Many species build pouch-formed hanging nests, which are very variable in form.

Bobolink, *Dolichonyx oryzivorus,* 6¾-7 in. Breeds in North America and winters in temperate parts of South America. Feeds on insects and seeds; often raids rice and other cereal plantations.

Cowbird, *Molothrus ater,* 7¾ in. Found in temperate North America. It often catches insects on the backs of cattle. The eggs are laid in other birds' nests, where the young grow up together with the nest clutch.

(from left) Bobolink; Cowbird; Red-breasted Starling; Baltimore Oriole

(above) Great Crested Cacique
(below) Yellow-rumped Cacique

Honeycreepers

The honeycreepers, Coerebidae, consist of about 40 species of small birds which are exclusively found in forests and gardens in tropical America from Mexico to Brazil. They feed on honey, soft fruits and insects. The tongue is incurved along the edges, and ends in a cleft-tip, and is well designed for sucking nectar. The nest is saucer-formed or spherical, with a side entrance, and is fixed to branches.

Mexican Diglossa, *Diglossa baritula*, 5 in., has a long beak with a small thin hook at the end, with which it pierces flowers in order to get at the nectar within; it also feeds on insects and spiders.

Blue Honeycreeper, *Cyanerpes cyaneus*, 4¾ in. Breeds in northern South America. In addition to nectar it also takes insects from flowers. The female builds a saucer-formed nest and lays two eggs.

Red-brested Starling, *Pezites militaris*, 9¾ in. Found in Peru, Chile and Argentina.

Baltimore Oriole, *Icterus galbula*, 7¼ in. Breeds in east North America and winters in Central America. It is often kept as a cage bird.

Great Crested Cacique, *Ostinops decumanus*, 17 in. Breeds in the forests of northern South America, and feeds on mice, lizards, insects and juicy fruits. The hanging pouch-like nest is about 2½ ft. long.

Yellow-rumped Cacique, *Cacicus cela*, 11¾ in. Sings continuously and is a good mimic.

(above) Mexican Diglossa
(below) Blue Honeycreeper

Hawaiian Honeycreepers

The Hawaiian honeycreepers, Drepanididae, used to have about 22 species. They occur exclusively in the Hawaii Islands, where there are otherwise only nine species of passerines, apart from a number of small birds which have been introduced. The Hawaiian honeycreepers are small to medium-sized birds, and most have a long thin beak and a tubular tongue with a brush-like tip. The feathers were once used in their thousands in the preparation of the Hawaiian royal robes. Nowadays the species are either extinct or very rare, not so much on the ground of the collecting of feathers, as because of the destruction of forests and the spread of disease from introduced birds.

Iiwi, *Vestiaria coccinea,* 6 in., has a long curved beak, which is inserted in the flowers of a myrtle tree, in order to get at nectar and insects.

Akialoa, *Hemignathus obscurus,* 5 in. This species also sucks nectar, but in addition uses the peculiar upper beak and the tongue for catching insects.

(from above) Snow Finch; Rock Sparrow; House Sparrow; Tree Sparrow

(above) Iiwi
(below) Akialoa

Weaver Birds

The weaver birds, Ploceidae, consist of some 720 species. They are nearly all small birds, mostly found in Africa but not in America except where introduced. They have a cone-shaped beak well adapted for cracking the shells of seeds, which form their principal food. The nests are often very complex and many are woven out of pieces of grass, straw or palm leaf fibre; the spherical or bottle-shaped nests usually have long entrance tunnels. Most weaver birds breed in colonies with the nests close to each other. Some are woodland birds, but most go about in flocks in open country. Such large flocks may do considerable damage in cornfields and many are

therefore ruthlessly hunted. During the breeding season, however, they are useful because they catch injurious insects as food for their young. In addition there are some weaver birds which are entirely insect eaters. The males most often have beautifully coloured plumage but the females are usually drabber in colour. The weaver birds may be divided into 5 subfamilies, the sparrows, whydahs, the true weavers, the buffalo weavers and the waxbills, which are often put into a family on their own.

Snow Finch, *Montifringilla nivalis,* 7 in. A mountain bird with a restricted distribution in the Pyrenees, Alps, Balkans and west Asia.

Rock Sparrow, *Petronia petronia,* 5½ in. Found in south Europe, north Africa and west Asia. It has a characteristic yellow patch on the throat.

House Sparrow, *Passer domesticus,* 5¾ in. Widespread over nearly the whole of Europe, North Africa and temperate Asia, living mostly in the neighbourhood of inhabited places. The male has a black throat, a dark grey or brown crown and its plumage is more mottled than that of the female. Sparrows feed particularly on wheat and oats, but also take many insects, especially during the breeding season. It has been introduced into Australia and America.

Tree Sparrow, *Passer montanus,* 5½ in. Found in most of Europe, with races extending to east Asia. The white cheeks have a black patch, the crown is chocolate-brown and the sexes are alike.

Paradise Whydah, *Steganura paradisaea,* 5½-6 in.; with the tail the male is 14 in. Found in Africa south of the Sahara.

Red-naped Whydah, *Coliuspasser laticauda,* 20 in. Found in Abyssinia and south-east Sudan.

Pin-tailed Whydah, *Vidua macroura,* 4 in., but the breeding male is 12 in.

(from above) Paradise Whydah;
Red-naped Whydah;
Pin-tailed Whydah; Social Weaver

Found in Africa south of the Sahara. It lays its eggs in the nests of waxbills and is polygamous. Feeds mainly on seeds.

Social Weaver, *Philetairus socius,* 5½ in. Found on the savannas of south Africa and very similar to the male common sparrow. They build large communal nests, in which each pair has its own compartment under one roof. Sometimes two hundred pairs may nest together.

Baya Weaver, *Ploceus hypoxanthus,* 5½ in. Found in India and south-east Asia; there are several races.

Buffalo Weaver, *Bubalornis albirostris,* 9¾ in. Often goes about in flocks following buffalo and cattle, to catch insects which are turned up by the animals. They gather together and build a nest complex, each pair with its own chamber.

Red Bishop, *Euplectes orix,* 5½ in. Found in tropical and southern Africa.

Java Sparrow, *Padda oryzivora,* 5-5½ in. Originally a native of Java and Sumatra, but now found in Asia, south China and introduced in the coastal parts of east Africa. Feeds on seeds, doing damage in rice fields.

Red-cheeked Cordon-bleu, *Uraeginthus bengalus,* 4¾ in. Found in tropical

(from left) Baya Weaver; Buffalo Weaver; Red Bishop

Africa from Senegal to Sudan, and commonly kept as a cage bird.

Crimson Finch, *Neochmia phaeton,* 4¾ in. Found across north Australia, it builds a bottle-shaped nest out of grass and leaves, most often in bushes.

Red-headed Finch, *Amadina erythrocephala,* 5-5½ in. Occurs in southern Africa, and feeds mainly on seeds, but also takes insects.

(from left) Java Sparrow; Red-cheeked Cordon-Bleu; Crimson Finch; Red-headed Finch

13

Finches and Buntings

The finches and buntings, Fringillidae, are a family of about 425 small to medium-sized birds. Most of them resemble sparrows, and at one time the sparrows were indeed classified together with the finches; nowadays, however, it is generally agreed that the sparrows belong among the weaver birds, particularly in view of their nest-building habits. The beak of the finches is usually thick and cone-shaped, and the upper mandible is often a little longer than the lower one. The edge of the lower beak is sharp and slightly incurved, and the whole structure is well designed for cracking seeds. The male and the female resemble each other except in the breeding season. The finches are most common in South America and the temperate regions of the northern hemisphere, but are not found in Australia or the Antarctic. They feed principally on seeds, fruits and buds, but many of them also take insects, particularly for feeding to the young. Most finches live in trees and many are good singers, some very good. The canaries, for example, occur wild as yellow-green birds on the Canaries, Madeira and the Azores and domesticated in a number of pure yellow and somewhat larger forms, which are even better singers.

Finches nearly always build a saucer-shaped nest, most often in trees and bushes, but sometimes on the ground or in rock crevices. The nest is built only by the female and it is only exceptionally that the male takes part in the incubation; however he feeds the female during incubation, and they both help to feed the young. Nearly all finches are monogamous, and during the breeding season the pair keeps to itself; later on the families join together into large flocks and may do damage in cornfields.

(from above) Chaffinch; Brambling; Snow Bunting; Lapland Bunting; Bullfinch

The finches may be divided into three groups: the true finches, the buntings and the cardinals, each with well over 100 species.

Chaffinch, *Fringilla coelebs*, 6 in. Widespread over nearly the whole of Europe and north Africa, extending into west Asia. Lives in woods, gardens and hedges, feeding on seeds, particularly mast, and also on insects, buds and berries. It builds its beautiful nest up in trees out of moss, grass and roots, camouflaged externally with leaves and lichen and lined internally with feathers and hairs.

Brambling, *Fringilla montifringilla*, 5¾ in. Breeds in the birch and conifer forests of Scandinavia eastwards to Altai in Asia, and winters in Europe south to the Mediterranean, and in south-west Asia.

Snow Bunting, *Plectrophenax nivalis*, 6½ in. Breeds in Scandinavia, Iceland and Scotland, and in many parts of the Arctic, and migrates southwards in autumn. The nest is built among boulders on mountains.

Lapland Bunting, *Calcarius lapponicus*, 6 in. Breeds on high ground in many parts of the Arctic, and migrates south in autumn. There is a very long claw on the back toe.

Bullfinch, *Pyrrhula pyrrhula*, 5¾ in. Found in the woods of north and central Europe and in the northern parts of Asia. The glossy blue-black skullcap occurs in both sexes, but the male is rose-red on the belly, the female brown. They feed on seeds and buds, often doing damage in orchards.

Redpoll, *Carduelis flammea*, 5 in. Breeds in the northern forests of Europe, Asia and America, wintering to the south. It feeds mostly on birch and alder seeds. The Mealy Redpoll is the paler, greyer Continental form whilst Britain has the smaller, browner Lesser Redpoll. Greenland also has a subspecies.

(from above) Redpoll; Linnet; Arctic Redpoll; Twite; Siskin; Goldfinch; Greenfinch

(above) Corn Bunting; Reed Bunting; *(below)* Cirl Bunting; Ortolan Bunting

Linnet, *Carduelis cannabina*, 5¼ in. Found in summer and winter throughout Europe, except in the northernmost regions, with allied forms in north-west Africa and west Asia. Frequents the edges of woods, copses and fields, and feeds on seeds, berries and insects.

Arctic Redpoll, *Carduelis hornemanni*, 5 in. Breeds in the high Arctic north of the tree zone. The rump is white and unstreaked.

Twite, *Carduelis flavirostris*, 5¼ in. Breeds in the British Isles and Norway; there are allied forms in central Asia.

Siskin, *Carduelis spinus*, 4¾ in. Breeds in Scotland, Ireland, and parts of north Europe, and winters to the south.

Goldfinch, *Carduelis carduelis*, 4¾ in. Breeds throughout the whole of Europe, except north Scandinavia, and also in north Africa and west Asia. It feeds on seeds, especially of thistles, and on insects.

Greenfinch, *Chloris chloris*, 5¾ in. Breeds in the same areas as the Goldfinch. Frequents gardens and the edges of woods, and feeds on seeds of corn and weeds and also takes buds, insects and spiders.

(above) Yellowhammer; Rustic Bunting; *(below)* Little Bunting; Yellow-breasted Bunting

Corn Bunting, *Emberiza calandra,* 7 in. Found in Europe as far north as south Scandinavia, and in north Africa and west Asia. The nest is built among grass and weeds and the food consists mainly of seeds and buds, with some insects.

Reed Bunting, *Emberiza schoeniclus,* 6 in. Breeds throughout Europe and north Asia, eastwards to Japan, in areas with swamps and reed-beds. Feeds on seeds of marsh plants, grasses, and on insects, crustaceans and molluscs.

Cirl Bunting, *Emberiza cirlus,* 6½ in. Found in west and south Europe, the Caucasus and Asia Minor.

Ortolan Bunting, *Emberiza hortulana,* 6½ in. Breeds in most of Europe, except Britain, as well as in west Asia. It feeds on seeds and insects and usually builds its nest on the ground among tall vegetation.

Yellowhammer, *Emberiza citrinella,* 6½ in. Breeds over nearly the whole of Europe and in north Asia. It lives in open country with scattered vegetation and builds a nest close to the ground in bushes and small trees.

Rustic Bunting, *Emberiza rustica,* 6 in. Found from north Scandinavia, through Siberia to China and Japan.

Little Bunting, *Emberiza pusilla,* 5¼ in. Breeds in marshy areas in north Russia and Siberia.

Yellow-breasted Bunting, *Emberiza aureola,* 5½ in. Breeds in birch and willow scrub in Finland, north Russia and Siberia.

Scarlet Grosbeak, *Carpodacus erythrinus,* 5¾ in. Breeds in swampy woodland from Finland to Siberia, and is only rarely seen in west Europe.

Crimson-collared Grosbeak, *Rhodothraupis celaeno,* 7¾ in. Found in Mexico.

Evening Grosbeak, *Hesperiphona vespertina,* 7¾ in. Found in North America east of the Rockies.

(from above) Scarlet Grosbeak; Crimson-collared Grosbeak; Evening Grosbeak; Pine Grosbeak; Hawfinch; Crossbill; Parrot-crossbill

(from above) Red Cardinal;
Red-crested Cardinal; Arizona Pyrrhuloxia

Parrot-crossbill, *Loxia pytyopsittacus,*
7 in. Breeds in the conifer forests of
north-east Europe and feeds on spruce
and larch seeds. Only rarely recorded in
Britain.

Red Cardinal, *Richmondena cardinalis,*
8¾ in. Found in the United States, with
related forms extending south to northern South America. The male is bright
red and the female olive-grey. Both sexes
are remarkably good singers. They con-
sume large numbers of injurious insects
and larvae and also take seeds and berries.
In spring and summer they live in pairs,
later they go about in flocks with the
young. In hard winters they migrate
southwards.

Red-crested Cardinal, *Paroaria cucullata,*
7¼ in. Found along the shores of the large
rivers in southern Brazil, Bolivia and the
Argentine.

Arizona Pyrrhuloxia, *Pyrrhuloxia sinu-
ata,* 7¼ in. Found in the south-western
United States and north Mexico. Feeds
on weed seeds, caterpillars and grasshoppers.

Pine Grosbeak, *Pinicola enucleator,* 8 in.
Breeds in conifer forests from Norway
to Kamtchatka and in western North
America. It feeds on seeds, buds and
berries, and has the tip of the upper beak
bent down into a hook.

Hawfinch, *Coccothraustes coccothraustes,*
7 in. Breeds in open woodland in the
greater part of Europe and Asia, including Britain. Feeds on the kernels of
cherry and plum stones, which it cracks
with the bill.

Crossbill, *Loxia curvirostra,* 6½ in. Breeds
in large parts of Europe (rarely in
Britain), central Asia, north-west Africa
and north America. Feeds on spruce,
pine and other conifer seeds, and on
berries and small insects.

(above) Blue Tanager
(below) Crimson-collared Tanager

Tanagers

The tanagers are a family of some 200 small to medium-sized birds, which live in America from south Canada to Argentina, Bolivia and Peru; they are particularly characteristic of tropical South America. The plumage is brilliant and gay, especially among the males. As a rule the female builds the nest alone and incubates the young.

Blue Tanager, *Thraupis episcopus,* 7 in. Lives on the edges of woods and in gardens and is known from Mexico to Peru. Unlike most tanagers the male and female are almost the same in appearance.
Crimson-collared Tanager, *Phlogothraupis sanguinolenta,* 7 in. Found from Mexico to Panama.
Three-coloured Tanager, *Tangara tricolor,* 4¾ in. Found in northern South America, mainly in Brazil.
Red-throated Ant Tanager, *Phoenicothraupis gutturalis,* 7¼ in. Found in central and northern South America.

(from above) Black-throated Green Warbler; Yellow Warbler; Audubon's Warbler

(above) Three-coloured Tanager
(below) Red-throated Ant Tanager

Wood Warblers

The wood warblers, Parulidae, are an entirely American family with some 110 small species distributed from Alaska to Argentina. Most of them live in trees and bushes, and they all feed on insects; in most cases this is their only food, so that they are very useful birds. The North American species winter in the tropics.

Yellow Warbler, *Dendroica petechia,* 5 in. Breeds from Canada to the West Indies.
Black-throated Green Warbler, *Dendroica virens,* 4¼ in. Found in eastern North America, mostly in conifer woods where it also nests.

(from above) Black-and-white Warbler;
Yellowthroat; American Redstart

Accentors or Hedge-sparrows

The accentors, Prunellidae, are a small
family of about 12 species which live in
Europe and north Asia. They differ from
sparrows in having a more slender beak.
Their main food is insects, but in winter
they feed on seeds.

Hedge Sparrow, *Prunella modularis,*
5¾ in. Breeds in the greater part of
Europe and west Asia, mostly in hedges
and open woodland.
Mountain Accentor, *Prunella montanella,*
5¾ in. Breeds in Siberia, and feeds mostly
on the ground.
Alpine Accentor, *Prunella collaris,* 7 in.
Breeds in the mountains of south and
central Europe, often up to the snow-
line. The nest is built in rough ground
on mountain slopes.

Audubon's Warbler, *Dendroica audu-
boni,* 5 in. It breeds in western America
from south Canada to California and
Arizona, and lives particularly in Doug-
las firs and catches insects in the air
like the flycatchers.
Black-and-white Warbler, *Mniotilta
varia,* 5½ in. Breeds in eastern north
America. Creeps around on the boles of
trees searching for insects.
Yellowthroat, *Geothlypis trichas,* 5 in.
Breeds in north and central America
and the West Indies. There are several
subspecies within this range.
American Redstart, *Setophaga ruticilla,*
5 in. Widespread in north America
and northern South America. A lively
bird, always on the hunt for insects
among bushes and in low trees. It builds
a saucer-shaped nest in the fork of a
tree, using grass and strips of bark held
together with spider silk.

(above) Hedge Sparrow
(centre) Mountain Accentor
(below) Alpine Accentor

(*above*) Ochre-crowned Pepper Shrike
(*below*) Red-eyed Vireo

(*above*) Black-fronted White-eye
(*below*) Vaal River White-eye

Vireos

The vireos, Vireonidae, consist of some 50 small American birds, mostly from tropical America.

Ochre-crowned Pepper Shrike, *Cyclarhis gujanensis*, 5¼ in., is found in scrubland on the edge of woods and rivers from Mexico and through South America to Chile. They prey on insects and larvae.

Red-eyed Vireo, *Vireo olivaceus*, 5½ in. Breeds from Canada to Florida and winters in central and south America. A good singer that is common in gardens, parks and woodland glades.

White-eyes

The white-eyes, Zosteropidae, are a mainly tropical family consisting of some 85 greenish-brown warbler-like birds, all very similar in appearance. They get their name from the tiny silky-soft white feathers which form a ring around the eye. They are widely distributed from Senegal in the west to the Fiji Islands in the east, and from Japan in the north to Tasmania and New Zealand in the south. They live mostly in the tree-tops, where they move about after insects, but they also take nectar, fruits and seeds.

Black-fronted White-eye, *Zosterops delicatula*, 4¾ in. Found in the mountain regions of eastern New Guinea.

Vaal River White-eye, *Zosterops vaalensis*, 4¾ in. Found only on the River Vaal in south Transvaal and northern Orange Free State.

Flowerpeckers

The flowerpeckers, Dicaeidae, are a family of over 50 rather small birds, which are found distributed from India to Australia and New Guinea. They live high up in the tops of trees, where they move about actively among the branches. As a rule

(*above*) Scarlet-backed Flowerpecker
(*below*) Spotted Diamond-bird

for collecting nectar; they also take insects.

Greyish-brown Honey-eater, *Meliphaga cinerea*, 8¾ in. Found in the mountain forests of New Guinea.
Sanguineous Honey-eater, *Myzomela sanguinolenta*, 4¾ in. Found in eastern Australia, where it is also known as the Bloodbird. The female is brownish.
Tui, *Prosthemadera novaeseelandiae*, 13¼ in. Found in the forests of New Zealand, living mainly in the tree-tops. Characterised by the tuft of curly white feathers on the neck. It is a remarkably fine singer and feeds on nectar, berries and insects.
New Guinea Friar Bird, *Philemon novae-guinea*, 15¾ in. Found in New Guinea. The sides of the head behind the eye are black and naked.

they go about in small flocks. Their food consists of insects, nectar, berries and other soft fruits.

Scarlet-backed Flowerpecker, *Dicaeum cruentatum*, 3 in. Found in south-east Asia, where it lives in the tops of trees and feeds mainly on berries. The pouch-like nest hangs down from a thin branch and has an opening towards the top on one side.
Spotted Diamond-bird, *Pardalotus punctatus*, 3½ in. Widely distributed in east and south Australia. It digs a tunnel almost 18 in. long in a bank and builds a nest at the end.

Honey-eaters

The honey-eaters, Meliphagidae, are a family of 162 small to medium-sized birds, found in the Pacific from New Zealand in the south and to Celebes in the west. They feed mostly on nectar and berries. The long narrow tongue forms a tube, split up at the end into filaments, so that it works like a brush

(*from above*) Greyish-brown Honey-eater;
Sanguineous Honey-eater; Tui;
New Guinea Friar Bird

Sunbirds

The sunbirds, Nectariniidae, consist of over 100 small birds from Africa, Asia and Australia, of which more than half are African. In most species the males have metallic colours, whilst the females are brown or greenish. The narrow extensible tongue forms a tube which divides into two at the tip and is used for collecting nectar. Sometimes they cheat by pricking a hole in the bottom of the flower and in this way neglect to pollinate flowers. The pouch-formed nest hangs on thin twigs and has a side entrance with a small porch. The female alone builds the nest, incubates the eggs and as a rule is also alone in feeding the young.

(above) Larger-streaked Spider Hunter
(below) Yellow-backed Sunbird

Malachite Sunbird, *Nectarinia famosa,*

(fr. above) Malachite Sunbird; Southern Double-collared Sunbird; Yellow-breasted Sunbird

6¾ in. Found in east and south Africa, mostly on scrub and moor at heights of 5,000-15,000 ft. The young are fed at first with regurgitated food, later with insect larvae, spiders and nectar.
Southern Double-collared Sunbird, *Cinnyris chalybeus,* 4¼ in. Found in the woods of Africa south of the Equator.
Yellow-breasted Sunbird, *Cinnyris frenata,* 4¾ in. Found in Celebes, Moluccas, and New Guinea to north-east Australia.
Larger-streaked Spider Hunter, *Arachnothera magna,* 7 in. Found in the teak forests of India and Burma, where, as the name suggests, it feeds principally on spiders.
Yellow-backed Sunbird, *Aethopyga siparaja,* 5½ in. Found in India and south-east Asia, including Sumatra. An active restless bird of the damp forests which feeds on nectar and insects.

Creepers

The creepers, Certhiidae, are small active birds of the northern hemisphere; there are six species.

Tree Creeper; Short-toed Tree Creeper

Tree Creeper, *Certhia familiaris,* 5 in.
Breeds in coniferous and deciduous
woods in most of Europe, in Asia and
North America. It runs up the stems of
trees, usually in a spiral.
Short-toed Tree Creeper, *Certhia brachydactyla,* 5 in. Breeds in central and
south Europe and along the coast of
the Mediterranean. The bill is longer
and the claws shorter than in the tree
creeper.

Wall Creeper

Nuthatches

The nuthatches, Sittidae, consist of about
30 small birds which are widely distributed in Europe, Asia, Australia and
north and central America. They are
perhaps the cleverest of all climbing
birds, and the only ones which can move
down a tree trunk head downwards.
They also climb along the upper and
under sides of perpendicular branches.
They feed mostly on insects and spiders;
most also take a certain amount of nuts
and fruit.

Wall Creeper, *Tichodroma muraria,* 6½ in.
Sometimes included among the tree
creepers. Breeds in the mountains of
Europe, Asia and north America at
heights of 2,000 to 9,000 ft. It climbs up
perpendicular cliff walls with the wings
half spread out, looking for insects and
spiders.

Nuthatch, *Sitta europaea,* 5½ in. Breeds in
Europe, including England, and through
Asia to the Pacific. It is a woodland bird
which keeps particularly to oak woods
and runs up and down the stems hunting
for insects and larvae; it also eats acorns
and hazel nuts, which it wedges fast in
bark crevices and then hacks open with
its strong bill. It nests in hollow trees
or deserted woodpecker holes; if the
entrance hole is too large it plasters mud
around the edges.
Brown-headed Nuthatch, *Sitta pusilla,*
4¼ in. Lives in forests of eastern North
America from Missouri and Delaware
to the Gulf States.
Corsican Nuthatch, *Sitta whiteheadi,*
4¾ in. Confined to the forests and mountain scrub of Corsica.
Velvet-fronted Nuthatch, *Sitta frontalis,*
5 in. Found in India, Malaya and Indonesia.
White-breasted Nuthatch, *Sitta carolinensis cookei,* 5½ in. Found in North

(above) Nuthatch; Brown-headed Nuthatch
(below) Corsican Nuthatch; <u>Velvet-fronted Nuthatch</u>; White-breasted Nuthatch

America from south Canada to south Mexico. It breeds in tree holes or deserted woodpecker holes, but does not use mud to reduce the size of the entrance.

Tits

The tits, Paridae, are a family of 65 small birds, none larger than a sparrow. The beak is short, the feet and claws strong; the male and female usually resemble each other. Tits are found widely distributed over the earth but are lacking in South America and the polar regions. The majority are found in the temperate regions of Europe and Asia. They are mostly woodland birds, which climb actively around on trees after insects and larvae. Many of them also eat berries and seeds and open the shells by holding them with one foot and hammering them apart with the beak. They are very trusting and often live in the immediate neighbourhood of man, in gardens and parks, and are willing to come to bird

(from left) <u>Great Tit</u>; Coal Tit; Blue Tit; Azure Tit

(above) Southern Black Tit
(below) Red-headed Tit

Great Tit, *Parus major,* 5½ in. Breeds in nearly the whole of Europe, Asia and north-west Africa. One of the largest species in the family, it lives mostly in deciduous woods, parks and gardens, and feeds on insects, larvae, worms, fruits and seeds. It nests in tree holes or in nesting boxes, but will also use holes in walls, drain-pipes, and flower-pots. The inside of the nest is lined with moss, hair, wool and feathers.

Coal Tit, *Parus ater,* 4¼ in. Breeds in nearly the whole of Europe, in Asia as far as the Himalayas and in north-west Africa, mostly in coniferous forests. It feeds on insects, larvae and seeds, particularly spruce seeds, and nests in hollow trees and old stumps.

Blue Tit, *Parus caeruleus,* 4½ in. Breeds throughout Europe except in the north, in west Asia and north-west Africa. It lives in deciduous woods and feeds on insects, larvae, fruit and seeds. The nest is often placed in holes in trees, and there may be 7-14 eggs.

Azure Tit, *Parus cyanus,* 5¼ in. Found in east Russia and Siberia, among willow trees and along streams, rivers and lakes. Occasionally strays to Europe.

tables. Most are resident, even where the winters are harsh, and it is not uncommon for many of the species to hoard winter food by storing cone-seeds, larvae and pupae in crevices in the bark. Most tits build nests of pieces of bark, moss, hair and feathers, in tree holes. Both parents help to feed the young.

(from left) Siberian Tit; Willow Tit; Long-tailed Tit; Crested Tit

Southern Black Tit, *Parus niger,* 6¼ in. Found in South Africa from the Zambesi to the Cape, usually in dry bush and woods.

Red-headed Tit, *Aegithaliscus concinnus,* 3¾ in. Distributed from India to China, mostly in the mountains at heights from 4,000 to 8,000 ft.

Siberian Tit, *Parus cinctus,* 5¼ in. Breeds in northern Scandinavia, north Russia and Siberia. It chips itself a nest hole in dead trees or takes over an old woodpecker hole.

Willow Tit, *Parus atricapillus,* 4½ in. Breeds in Europe, except the southwestern region, and in north Asia and north America. It feeds on insects and seeds.

Long-tailed Tit, *Aegithalos caudatus,* 5 in., of which 3 in. is tail. Breeds throughout most of Europe and north Asia, usually in thickets. The ovoid nest is built of leaves, moss and feathers with the opening near the top on one side. They feed exclusively on insects and larvae.

Crested Tit, *Parus cristatus,* 4½ in. Breeds in most parts of Europe and west Asia; in Britain it is confined to a small area of north-east Scotland. Nests in holes in trees.

Boreal Chickadee, *Parus hudsonicus,* 5½ in. Found in Canada and northern United States, where it breeds in spruce forests.

Tufted Tit, *Parus bicolor,* 6¼ in. Found in the eastern United States and from Florida to Nebraska to the west. In spite of its appearance it is not closely related to the crested tit. It lives in living or dead hollow trees and always uses hair to line the nest.

Penduline Tit, *Remiz pendulinus,* 4¼ in. Breeds in south-east Europe and further

(from above) Boreal Chickadee; Tufted Tit

eastwards to Japan, mostly in reed thickets and scrub along rivers, where it hunts for insects and larvae. The thin, pointed beak is used by the male to weave the pouch-formed nest, which usually hangs out over the water from a twig, and has a funnel-shaped entrance.

Penduline Tit

(from above) Bearded Tit; Heude's Crow-tit

Parrotbills

The parrotbills or crow-tits, Paradoxorn-ithidae, are a family of small tit-like birds found in Europe and Asia, most in India and South China. Many of them have a powerful almost parrot-like bill. They live in dense bushes and reed or bamboo thickets.

Bearded Tit, *Panurus biarmicus,* 6½ in. Distributed very unevenly in central and south Europe, extending through Asia to Japan; a few breed in eastern England. They live in reed-beds and feed on insects and reed seeds, and nest low down.

Heude's Crow-tit, *Paradoxornis heudei,* 6¼ in. Found in east China.

Picathartes

The Picathartidae are a West African family, with only two species. They are forest birds, which live on the ground and look rather like thin crows on long thrush-like legs; and they have naked heads. They fix their mud nests to rock faces 6-15 ft. high in woodland areas or else put them in crevices in cliffs. They hunt for insects and frogs in the neighbourhood of streams.

Cameroon Picathartes, *Picathartes oreas,* 15½ in. Found in the Cameroons in West Africa.

Guinea Picathartes, *Picathartes gymnocephalus,* 19½ in. Found locally in the forests of West Africa.

(above) Cameroon Picathartes
(below) Guinea Picathartes

(above) Superb Bird of Paradise; Blue Bird of Paradise
(below) King Bird of Paradise; Lawes' Six-plumed Bird of Paradise

Birds of Paradise

The birds of paradise, Paradisaeidae, are a family of 43 species, of which 38 live in the rain forests of New Guinea and the rest are distributed from the Moluccas to north Australia. The plumage of the females and the young birds is dullish and dark, but during the breeding season that of the males is strikingly beautiful. They are polygamous, and at the beginning of the mating time the males gather together in definite places to carry out their courtship display. At one time the skins were exported in tens of thousands, but nowadays the birds are strictly protected.

Superb Bird of Paradise, *Lophorina superba*, 9 in. Found in the forests of south-east New Guinea. There are two collars of feathers, one at the back and the other on the front of the throat; these are erected during courtship.

Blue Bird of Paradise, *Paradisornis rudolphi*, 11 in. Found in the southern mountainous regions of New Guinea. As do many others in the group, the male hangs head downwards during courtship.

King Bird of Paradise, *Cicinnurus regius*, 6¼ in. Found over the whole of New Guinea, living in low trees along the coasts. The white and metallic wing feathers can be spread downwards like fans, and the two middle thread-like tail feathers cross each other and have a small metallic green vane at the tip, which is spirally twisted. Its voice sounds like the mewing of a kitten.

Lawe's Six-plumed Bird of Paradise, *Parotia lawesi*, 12 in. Found in south-

29

west New Guinea. Three very long thread-like feathers come off at the back of each eye. The courtship dances take place on the ground, 6-8 males performing at a time.

Ribbon Tail, *Taeniaparadisea mayeri,* 39 in. Found in the forests of New Guinea. The two tail feathers are longer than in any other bird of paradise.

Meyer's Sickle-bill, *Epimachus meyeri,* 46 in. Lives in the mountain regions of New Guinea at heights of 7,000-9,000 ft.

Wallace's Bird of Paradise, *Semioptera wallacei,* 9½ in. This species occurs only on the islands of Batchian and Gilolo in the Moluccas.

Wilson's Bird of Paradise, *Diphyllodes respublica,* 6¾ in. The two central tail feathers are twisted and cross each other. During the mating dance the related

(left, from above) Ribbon Tail; Meyer's Sickle-bill; Wallace's Bird of Paradise; Wilson's Bird of Paradise; *(right, from above)* Lesser Bird of Paradise; Enamelled Bird

Magnificent Bird of Paradise clears the earth around a small tree and bites off some of the overhanging leaves. It then starts to dance and climbs up to the top of the tree where it displays with raised ornamental plumes.

Lesser Bird of Paradise, *Paradisea minor*, 14 in. Found in New Guinea and Jobi Island. The long veil-like ornamental plumes on the sides of the body are bright yellow. The middle tail feathers are thread-like and lengthened.

Enamelled Bird, *Pteridophora alberti*, 7½ in. Found in New Guinea. The two long nape feathers consist of a thread-like shaft which has over 30 small shiny enamel light blue horny plates along one side. The courtship display has not been observed.

Green Manucode, *Manucodia chalybata*, 15½ in. Found in the mountain regions of New Guinea. The male and the female resemble each other.

Trumpet Bird, *Phonygammus keraudrenii*, 13 in. Found in New Guinea and north Queensland.

Satin Bower-bird

Green Manucode; Trumpet Bird

Bower-birds

The bower-birds, Ptilonorhynchidae, are a family of about 19 species, which are found in New Guinea and Australia. They are related to the birds of paradise but have no ornamental plumes. They are, however, outstanding builders with an aesthetic sense and the ability to use tools. The males attract the females by building bowers, which they decorate. The bower or arena differs according to the species. Some merely clear a part of the forest floor as a dancing place, but most decorate the arena with colourful articles, lay out lawns and build bowers. These huts or bowers have nothing to do with the nests, which are built up in the trees. The decorations of the arena may consist of mollusc shells, seeds and fruist, feathers, stones, bits of paper, matchsticks, pieces of metal, bits of glass and threads. The best specialists paint

(from above) Green Cat-bird;
Great Grey Bower-bird; Golden Bird;
Yellow-crested Gardener

the outside of the bower. The male may take some 2-4 months in each year to build up and maintain the bower. The female comes to inspect it; and when everything is in order, she accepts his invitation and goes into the bower.

Satin Bower-bird, *Ptilonorhynchus violaceus*, 11½ in. Found in the damp forests of eastern Australia. It feeds mostly on fruits but also takes seeds and insects. In building the bower they clear an area of ground in the forest and build an arena of thin twigs and sticks, which are arranged so that they curve inwards and meet at the top. Near to it, and usually at one entrance, the male will also make a display ground, on which he strews a number of coloured objects, apparently at random. The bower usually takes him a day or two to build. In addition he will often paint the inside of the bower, using either fruit pulp from local berries or masticated charcoal mixed with spit.

Green Cat-bird, *Ailuroedus crassirostris*, 11¾ in. Found in the eastern part of Australia. It does not build a bower, but cleans a piece of ground which it decorates with flowers, berries and leaves; the voice is like the mewing of a cat.

Great Grey Bower-bird, *Chlamydera nuchalis*, 11 in. Found on open scrubland in tropical Australia.

Golden Bird, *Xanthomelus aureus*, 11¾ in. Found in New Guinea, this is one of the most beautiful of the bower-birds.

Yellow-crested Gardener, *Amblyornis macgregoriae*, 11 in. Found in the high mountain forests of New Guinea. It makes a large lawn of yellow-green moss which it decorates with berries and flowers. As soon as the flowers wither it replaces them with new ones.

Crows

The crows, Corvidae, are a family of some 100 species of powerfully built birds. They are found distributed over almost the whole of the earth from the polar regions to the tropics, except in New Zealand and certain Polynesian islands. Some crows are carnivorous, others vegetarian, but the majority are omnivorous.

Raven, *Corvus corax,* 25 in. This is the largest crow and—after the lyrebird—the largest of all the passerines. It is practically independent of climate and is found over nearly the whole of the northern hemisphere from the ice fields of Greenland to the deserts of Mexico, although it is now rare or extinct in France, Belgium, Holland, Germany and Denmark. Ravens feed mostly on rodents, insects, larvae, worms, young birds and carrion, as well as bivalve molluscs and stranded fish. The nest is built at the top of a high tree or on a cliff.

Jackdaw, *Corvus monedula,* 13 in. Found almost everywhere in Europe and west

(above) Raven
(below) Jackdaw

Asia. Easily distinguished by the ash-grey nape and the pearl-grey eyes. It feeds mostly on insects, larvae and corn and breeds in small colonies in buildings and hollow trees.

(from left) Pied Crow; Thick-billed Raven

(from left) Carrion Crow; Hooded Crow; Rook

Pied Crow, *Corvus albus*, 17½ in. Found almost throughout the whole of tropical Africa, and in Madagascar.

Thick-billed Raven, *Corvultur crassirostris*, 23 in. Found in the mountain regions of Eritrea and Abyssinia. It feeds mostly on carrion and garbage and lives in the neighbourhood of man.

Carrion Crow, *Corvus corone*, 18½ in. Breeds in west Europe, including Britain.

Carrion crows usually go about alone or in pairs, unlike rooks.

Hooded Crow, *Corvus cornix*, 18½ in. Breeds in north and east Europe, in Ireland and parts of Scotland. Hooded crows differ from the rook and carrion crow in having a grey back and underparts. They are almost omnivorous, feeding on insects, larvae, worms, carrion, mice, rats, young hares, young

(from left) Azure-winged Magpie; Magpie

birds, eggs, corn and potatoes. The nest is built high up in trees and often used for a number of years.

Rook, *Corvus frugilegus,* 18 in. Found in central Europe, westwards to Britain, northwards to south Norway and eastwards into Siberia. In the adult the skin round the root of the bill is naked, unlike the carrion crow. It feeds on insects, larvae and worms, and also on potatoes and sprouting corn. It nests in the tops of high trees in large colonies.

Azure-winged Magpie, *Cyanopica cyanus,* 13½ in. Breeds in Spain and Portugal as well as in eastern Siberia, China and Japan. It lives mostly in oak woods, olive groves and gardens.

Magpie, *Pica pica,* 18 in. Breeds throughout Europe as well as north Africa, north and central Asia and the western part of north America, and feeds on insects, larvae, worms and snails; it also raids the nests of small birds for eggs and young. The large, solid twiggy nests are usually built in high trees, often in the neighbourhood of houses and farms;

(left) Urraca Jay
(right, from above) Chough; Alpine Chough; Siberian Jay; Jay; Nutcracker

35

the nest is roofed over, with one or two entrances at the sides.

Urraca Jay, *Cyanocorax chrysops,* 14¼ in. Found in the forests of South America, where it goes about in flocks and may do a lot of damage on maize plantations.

Alpine Chough, *Pyrrhocorax graculus,* 15 in. Found in the Pyrenees, the Alps, the Balkans and in Asia as far as China. It has been observed at great heights on Mount Everest.

Chough, *Pyrrhocorax pyrrhocorax,* 15½ in.

(*above*) Blue Jay
(*centre*) Steller's Jay
(*below*) Black-throated Jay

Breeds locally in west Britain, Spain, the Alps, south Italy, the Balkans, and eastwards as far as China. It nests in cliff crevices and caves.

Siberian Jay, *Perisoreus infaustus,* 12 in. Breeds in conifer forests in north Europe and Asia, and feeds on cone seeds, berries, insects, snails and birds' eggs.

Jay, *Garrulus glandarius,* 13½ in. Breeds in the woodland areas of Europe, north Africa and north Asia. It is fond of acorns, but also eats mast, berries, corn, insects, larvae, worms, young birds and eggs. Although living well hidden among trees one often hears its raucous voice.

Nutcracker, *Nucifraga caryocatactes,* 12½ in. Breeds in large areas of Europe and Asia, mainly in conifer woods, and feeds mostly on hazel nuts and cone seeds. During the autumn it hides nuts and seeds as winter stores.

Blue Jay, *Cyanocitta cristata,* 11 in. Found in North America from Newfoundland in the north-east to Texas in the southwest and is most common in the eastern U.S.A. It lives chiefly in dense woodland, where it raids the nests of other birds for eggs and young. It also feeds on small mammals, amphibians, insects and larvae, fruits and seeds.

Steller's Jay, *Cyanocitta stelleri,* 12½ in. Found in the conifer forests of western America from Alaska to Nicaragua and eastwards to the Rocky Mountains.

Black-throated Jay, *Garrulus lanceolatus,* 13 in. Found in the Himalayas, where it breeds at heights of 5,000-8,000 ft.

Blue Pie, *Urocissa erythrorhyncha,* 25 in., has a tail measuring 15 in. Widespread in south-east Asia. It is very wary and gives its warning cry as soon as a predatory mammal or a bird of prey comes near. It feeds principally on insects and fruits and builds its nest in the trees,

either a little above the ground or very high up.

Green Magpie, *Cissa chinensis,* 15 in. Found in the Himalayas, parts of east India, and Burma.

Indian Tree-pie, *Dendrocitta vagabunda,* 17 in. Found in India and western parts of south-east Asia to the Himalayas, and common in the woods of northern India, where they live in pairs or in small flocks.

Hooded Tree-pie, *Crypsirina cucullata,* 17 in. Found in Siam and Burma.

Pander's Ground-jay, *Podoces panderi,* 9¾ in. Found in Turkestan and Transcaspia, particularly in the steppe and desert regions, where saxaul bushes flourish. They run fast on the ground but seldom fly.

(top) Blue Pie; Green Magpie; Indian Tree-pie
(right) Hooded Tree-pie; Pander's Ground-jay

Huia and Saddleback

The family Philesturnidae contains only two species, both restricted to New Zealand. Of these the Saddleback still survives on North Island.

Huia, *Heteralochus acutirostris,* 19-21 in. Not observed since 1907 and now extinct. The Maori chiefs used the beautiful tail feathers as ornaments. It hopped about actively, but would seldom fly. The male fed by chiselling insects and larvae out of holes in wood and when it could not reach the prey the female would haul it out with her long curved beak, a division of labour which is probably unique in the animal kingdom.

Kokakos

The family Callaeadidae, with two species, is restricted to New Zealand.

(from above) Black-backed Butcher Bird; Grey Bell Magpie; Black-backed Magpie

South Island Kokako, *Callaeas cinerea,* 15½ in. A flightless bird that feeds on buds, berries and insects.

Butcher Birds

The butcher birds, Cracticidae, are a family of some 13 species, found in open forest and tree-clad savanna in Australia and New Guinea. They are closely related to the crows, which they also resemble in size and colour.

Black-backed Butcher Bird, *Cracticus mentalis,* 17 in. Found in the east of Australia. It lives in the woods, but may also enter gardens or even houses. It feeds mostly on insects, which are taken on the ground. Peculiarly enough it has a predilection for using steel wire as a nest material.

(above) Huia, male and female
(below) South Island Kokako

Grey Bell Magpie, *Neostrepera versicolor*, 19½ in. Widespread in Australia and Tasmania. It feeds for the greater part on plant food and may do damage in fruit plantations.

Black-backed Magpie, *Gymnorhina tibicen*, 13½ in. Found in central and eastern Australia. It often sits up on a branch lying in wait for large insects, mostly beetles, which it catches and spits on thorns, rather in the manner of a shrike.

Drongos

The drongos, Dicruridae, are a family of about 20 species, occurring in Africa, India and Australia, where they live both in thick rain forests and out on the tree-clad savanna. They feed mostly on grasshoppers, dragonflies, cicadas, bees and spiders, but also eat fruits. They hunt the insects in the air or sit in wait on a branch, fly out and snap the prey and take it back to their starting point.

Square-tailed Drongo, *Dicrurus ludwigi*, 7¼ in. Found in thick scrub in East Africa from Somaliland to Natal.

Large Racket-tailed Drongo, *Dicrurus paradiseus*, 27 in., of which the outermost tail feathers are 13 in. long. Found in India, Ceylon and south-east Asia. In contrast to the other drongos it has a melodious voice.

Drongo, *Dicrurus adsimilis*, 9½ in. This, the commonest of the African drongos, is found over almost the whole of Africa south of the Sahara. It is known for its fearless behaviour in attacking larger birds. It feeds on insects which have been startled by savanna fires, and thinks nothing of following them into the smoke.

Hair-crested Drongo, *Dicrurus hottentottus*, 11½ in. Found in India and further east. The two outermost tail feathers are elongated and vary in form and size from area to area.

(from above) Square-tailed Drongo; Large Racket-tailed Drongo; Drongo; Hair-crested Drongo

Golden Oriole

Orioles

The orioles, Oriolidae, are a family of 34 starling-sized birds, which have their main distribution centre in Indonesia, whence they have spread westwards to India and Africa and southwards to Australia. In addition one species has reached northwards to Manchuria, whilst the Golden Oriole is the only species of

the family in Europe. Most orioles are woodland birds which live in the tops of the trees. In the majority it is only the males which have the brilliant plumage, whilst the females are as a rule inconspicuous. The voice consists of fluty notes and harsh warning screeches. They feed mostly on insects and larvae, but many also eat fruits.

Golden Oriole, *Oriolus oriolus,* 9½ in. Breeds everywhere in Europe except in Britain and most of Scandinavia, and also in north Africa and west Asia to India; it is a summer visitor to southeast England. Only the male is canary yellow, the female is olive-green on the upper side and greyish on the underparts with black oblong spots, and the young birds are mainly like the females. Like other members of the family the golden oriole prefers deciduous woods, living high up in the trees, particularly in beech and oak. It often comes down to the ground, but is difficult to see as it moves around among the branches; on the other hand one can often hear its beautiful voice. The male begins to sing before dawn and continues with small

(above) Black-headed Oriole; Yellow-bellied Fig-bird
(below) Yellow Oriole; Slender-billed Oriole

breaks up to noon and then starts again when the sun begins to set. The food consists mostly of insects and larvae. The deep saucer-formed nest is built high up on a tree branch and is made of grass, roots and bast and lined with wool and feathers.

Black-headed Oriole, *Oriolus larvatus,* 8½ in. Found in tropical east Africa and in Angola.

Yellow-bellied Fig-bird, *Sphecoteres flaviventris,* 15½ in. Found in the forests of north and north-east Australia; it feeds exclusively on fruits.

Yellow Oriole, *Oriolus flavicinctus,* 11½ in. Found in tropical northern Australia. It feeds on fruits.

Slender-billed Oriole, *Oriolus tenuirostris,* 10½ in. Widely distributed in India and south-east Asia, where it lives in open woods.

Starlings

The starlings, Sturnidae, are a family of about 120 species; the majority are found in tropical Africa and south Asia and only a few in north Asia and Europe. They have a smooth, glossy plumage and very pointed wings. As a rule the sexes resemble each other but the plumage of the young birds is very different. Most breed in tree holes and cliff crevices, often in large colonies.

Starling, *Sturnus vulgaris,* 8½ in. Found in Europe, except in the south of Spain and Italy, and in west Asia. The autumn plumage has a mass of white spots which disappear in the spring, so that the bird takes on a darker appearance. It lives mostly in open fields and near houses, often in city centres and feeds on insects, larvae, worms and soft fruits. The nest is built in tree holes, buildings

(from above) Starling;
Rose-coloured Starling;
Pied Myna; Jerdon's Starling

(from left) Cape Glossy Starling; Long-tailed Glossy Starling; Superb Starling

and nest-boxes. Many of the starlings in west Europe move northwards in autumn and winter. The species has been introduced into north America, Australia and New Zealand.

Rose-coloured Starling, *Sturnus roseus,* 8½ in. Breeds in central Asia and westwards to south-east Europe, sometimes in Italy and Hungary. At irregular intervals it undertakes long migrations and has been observed in all the countries of Europe. It has a distinctive crest and

the male is strikingly rose-pink, the female more grey-brown. It eats large numbers of migratory locusts. A sociable bird which sometimes gathers in thousands at the breeding places.

Pied Myna, *Sturnopastor contra,* 9 in. Widely distributed in India and southeast Asia. It feeds on insects, fruits and seeds, and is the best singer amongst the starlings.

Jerdon's Starling, *Sturnus burmanicus,* 10 in. Found in Burma. At night they

(above) Indian Grackle; Eastern Golden Grackle; *(below)* Common Myna; Wattled Starling

collect in communal roosts in sugar plantations and bamboo thickets.

Cape Glossy Starling, *Lamprocolius nitens,* 10 in. Found in scrub country in South Africa.

Long-tailed Glossy Starling, *Lamprotornis caudatus,* 19 in. The tail makes up over half of the length. Found in tropical west Africa and east to Sudan. The voice is harsh and raucous. It feeds on insects, fruits and seeds.

Superb Starling, *Spreo superbus,* 8¼ in. Common in north-east Africa. Its roofed-over spherical nest is found in the thorny trees on savanna.

Indian Grackle, *Gracula religiosa,* 9½ in. Found in India, Burma and Indonesia. It keeps to mountain forests and is principally a fruit-eater. An excellent cage bird, which may learn to whistle small tunes and mimic several different sounds.

Eastern Golden Grackle, *Melanopyrrhus orientalis,* 10¼ in. Found in parts of New Guinea.

Common Myna, *Acridotheres tristis,* 9¾ in. Widespread in India, Ceylon, Burma and parts of south-east Asia, mostly living in large flocks close to inhabited places. They feed mainly on grasshoppers and have been introduced into Africa and Australia.

Wattled Starling, *Creatophora cinerea,* 8¼ in. Found in Africa, where it breeds in enormous colonies in bushes and small trees and feeds mainly on locusts.

Waxwings

The waxwings, Bombycillidae, are a family of only 8 species. The short straight beak has a little indentation behind the hooked tip. The plumage is thick and soft, and there is a crest on the head which can be erected. They feed principally on fruits and go about

(from above) Waxwing; Phainopepla

during most of the year in large flocks.

Waxwing, *Bombycilla garrulus,* 7 in. Breeds in north Scandinavia, north Asia and north America; in Europe some move southwards and westwards in winter and are frequently seen in Britain. The secondary wing feathers end in a small waxy red plate. Waxwings are very sociable and during the breeding season they live mostly in conifer forests. The food consists principally of berries, but in summer they take many insects.

Phainopepla, *Phainopepla nitens,* 7¼ in. Found in the south-western United States from Texas to California, and in Mexico; the female is grey-brown. They feed on insects, but also eat some fruits. The male only builds the nest and he also takes part in incubation and in the rearing of the young.

(above) Ashy Swallow-shrike
(below) White-browed Swallow-shrike

Prevost's Vanga

Swallow-shrikes

The swallow-shrikes, Artamidae, are a
family of 10 species, which resemble
swallows more than starlings, although
not closely related to either. They have
long wings and powerful bills and are
found in south Asia, Indonesia and
Australia. They feed exclusively on
insects, which they hunt in flocks and
catch in the air. They spend the night
in crowded groups in trees. Many build
their nests at the base of palm leaves or
tree fern fronds. The nest is made of
roots, palm fibre, grass, moss and
feathers. The young are fed by both
parents and are cared for long after
they have left the nest.

Ashy Swallow-shrike, *Artamus fuscus,*
7 in. Found in India, Ceylon and Burma.
White-browed Swallow-shrike, *Arta-*
mus superciliosus, 7½ in. Found in
Australia, and often seen in large numbers on telephone wires.

Vangas

The vangas, Vangidae, are a family of
some 12 species, related to the shrikes
and the helmet-shrikes. They are found
exclusively in Madagascar, where as a
rule they go about in small flocks in the
rain forests and on the tree clad savanna.

Prevost's Vanga, *Euryceros prevosti,*
10¾ in., lives up in the tops of the trees
in small flocks and feeds on insects.

Shrikes

The shrikes, Laniidae, are a family of
some 70 species, which are found in
tropical and temperate regions, by far
the majority in Africa, only two in north
America and the remainder in Europe
and Asia. The powerful upper beak
is hooked at the tip. The shrikes may be
regarded as the birds of prey among the
passerines. They catch their prey in

the air or on the ground, piercing it with the beak, and letting it fall to the ground. There they seize it and then fly with it to a tree, and impale it on a thorn. The prey consists of small mammals, small birds, lizards, frogs and larger insects. Sometimes they have the prey hanging out, almost like a larder.

Great Grey Shrike, *Lanius excubitor*, 9½ in. Breeds over nearly the whole of Europe, and in north Africa, Asia and northern North America; some migrate to Britain in winter. They often live on the edges of woods, and will perch on the top of a bush or in a tree, spying out for prey. They feed on insects, frogs, lizards, mice, young birds and small birds. The larger prey is wedged fast in the fork of a branch or spitted on a thorn before it is pulled apart.

Red-backed Shrike, *Lanius collurio*, 6¾ in. Breeds throughout Europe, except in the north, and in west Asia. The female is brownish on the upper side and whitish or buff below with narrow dark cross-stripes. The male is a good singer and can mimic the voices of other birds. Red-backed shrikes live on bushy heaths, in plantations, gardens and hedges and feed on dung-beetles, butterflies, grasshoppers, dragonflies and other insects. They nest in bushes and small trees.

Woodchat Shrike, *Lanius senator*, 6¾ in. Breeds in central and south Europe and in north Africa, usually in woods, thickets, gardens, and olive groves. It is a good singer and a very clever mimic. It feeds almost exclusively on insects, particularly beetles and bumble-bees.

Masked Shrike, *Lanius nubicus*, 6¾ in. Distributed in west Asia, with a few extending to the Balkans, and living in

(from above) Great Grey Shrike; Red-backed Shrike; Woodchat Shrike; Masked Shrike; Black-headed Shrike

(above) Crimson-breasted Shrike
(below) Grey-headed Bush-shrike

family of some 12 species, which are close to the shrikes and are characterised by having a ring of skin around the eye and as a rule a crest on the head. The family is widespread in Africa south of the Sahara. They feed mostly on larger insects, but sometimes also eat fruits.

Straight-crested Helmet-shrike, *Prionops plumata*, 8¼ in. The feathers on the forehead grow upwards like a brush. They often occur in small flocks, which hunt insects in the trees or on the ground; they make a continual snapping noise with the beak whilst hunting. The nest is built of bark, grass and pieces of root and usually placed up in the fork of a tree.

Yellow-crested Helmet-shrike, *Prionops alberti*, 7¾ in. Found only in the eastern part of the Congo and first observed in 1932.

meadows and olive groves. In habits it resembles the preceding species.

Black-headed Shrike, *Lanius nigriceps*, 10½ in. Found in Asia.

Crimson-breasted Shrike, *Laniarius atrococcineus*, 9 in. Found in dry scrubland in the Kalahari Desert and southwards to the Orange River. It builds a flat nest of pieces of bark, plant fibre and roots.

Grey-headed Bush-shrike, *Malaconotus blanchoti*, 10½ in. The largest of all the shrikes, it and the last species belong among the African bush-shrikes, which are found in savanna scrub; they do not spit their prey on thorns.

Helmet-shrikes

The helmet-shrikes, Prionopidae, are a

(above) Yellow-crested Helmet-shrike
(below) Straight-crested Helmet-shrike

(above) Yellow Shrike-robin
(below) Black-tailed Thickhead

Whistlers

The whistlers, Pachycephalidae, are a family of about 20 species from Indonesia, New Guinea and Australia. They are closely related to the flycatchers and have a melodious piping voice.

Yellow Shrike-robin, *Eopsaltria placens*, 7 in. Found in east and south Australia and in New Guinea. Feeds on insects and larvae.

Black-tailed Thickhead, *Pachycephala melanura*, 7 in. Found in northern Australia and New Guinea, usually in woods along the coast and in mangrove swamps, where it hunts for insects in the mud left by the falling tide. The tail is blacker than shown in the illustration.

Flycatchers

The flycatchers, Muscicapidae, are a family of about 400 species, which are very variable amongst themselves, and related both to the shrikes and to the thrushes. They are found in the Old World, particularly in the tropics. They live among trees and are all insectivorous; they usually fly out from a high branch, catch the prey in the air and then return to their starting point. As a rule the beak is short and flat with long bristles at its root.

Spotted Flycatcher, *Muscicapa striata*, 5½ in. Breeds throughout Europe, and also in north Africa and west Asia. The female resembles the male but is a little paler. They live in high trees in forest clearings and parks, where they sit on

(above) Spotted Flycatcher
(below, from left) Collared Flycatcher;
Pied Flycatcher; Red-breasted Flycatcher

(above) Paradise Flycatcher;
Cape Paradise Flycatcher
(below) Black-chinned Monarch Flycatcher;
Black-naped Monarch Flycatcher

on buildings or trees, sometimes behind creepers. The nest material consists of straw, leaves, moss and roots, and the inside is lined with hair, feathers, down and wool. Both parents help to incubate the eggs and feed the young.

Collared Flycatcher, *Muscicapa albicollis,* 5 in. Breeds in eastern central Europe and further east into Asia Minor, and is sometimes seen as a summer visitor in west Europe. They resemble the pied flycatcher in habits, but the voice of the male is more powerful.

Pied Flycatcher, *Muscicapa hypoleuca,* 5 in. Breeds in most of Europe, except south Italy, Spain and the Balkans, as well as in north Africa and west Asia. The female is olive brown above and greyish or buff underneath and the wings and tail are brownish black with white as in the male; in winter the male has a similar plumage. They live in open woods, parks and gardens, and resemble the spotted flycatcher in feeding habits. They build in hollow trees, but are also willing to breed in nest-boxes. The nest is made of grass, small roots and bast fibres and is lined with horsehair and feathers. The male has a strong melodious voice.

Red-breasted Flycatcher, *Muscicapa parva,* 4½ in. Breeds in Germany and central Europe, as well as in Asia; it has been seen occasionally in Britain as a passage migrant. The female does not have the orange throat. A shy bird that is difficult to find as it lives well hidden in the tree-tops. The nest is built on trees, in the clefts of branches or sometimes on cliff ledges, usually rather high up, and is made of moss, grass and hair. The eggs are incubated by the female and the young are fed with insects by both parents.

Paradise Flycatcher, *Terpsiphone paradisi,* 14 in. Found in most of India and

the lookout for insects. Before taking off they make a quick bow or curtsey and flick the wings and tail. Like the other flycatchers they seldom come down to the ground. The nest may be built

(*above*) Brubru Shrike; Fiscal Flycatcher
(*below*) White-browed Fantail Flycatcher; New Guinea Broadbill

eastern Asia. As in the other paradise flycatchers it has a crest on the head, and in the males the central tail feathers are much elongated. The females are brown and not so long in the tail; some of the males may also be brown like the females, but they always have the characteristic long tail.

Cape Paradise Flycatcher, *Terpsiphone perspicillata,* 9-16 in. Found in the eastern parts of south Africa in woods along the rivers. In the male the two middle feathers of the tail are much elongated.

Black-chinned Monarch Flycatcher, *Monarcha frater,* 7 in. Found in the mountain forests of New Guinea.

Black-naped Monarch Flycatcher, *Hypothymis azurea,* 6½ in. Widespread in south-east Asia, living on the edges of forests and in bamboo thickets. It feeds on insects, but does not fly out to catch them in the air.

Brubru Shrike, *Nilaus brubru,* 6¼ in. Found on the savannas of south-east Africa.

Fiscal Flycatcher, *Sigelus silens,* 5 in. Found in South Africa.

White-browed Fantail Flycatcher, *Rhipidura aureola,* 7 in. Found in India and Burma, where it is common in the woods.

New Guinea Broadbill, *Peltops blainvillii,* 7¼ in. Found in New Guinea, living in the tree-tops.

Warblers

The warblers, Sylviidae, are a family of over 300 species of small insect-eating birds with elongated bodies and thin beaks. About two-thirds of the species are found in Africa, the remainder in Europe, Asia and Australia, apart from a few in North America. They live among trees, bushes or reeds and hunt among leaves and twigs for insects

49

which are almost their sole food; the northern species may, however, take some berries. Many of the species lack characteristic pattern, and the plumage becomes very worn so that in the latter part of the year they may be difficult to distinguish, except by their songs which differ widely and are very beautiful. The majority of warblers from the temperate zone are migratory.

Whitethroat, *Sylvia communis,* 5½ in. Found throughout Europe except in the far north, as well as in north-west Africa and in a large part of Asia. It lives mainly in hedges and on the edges of woods and favours thorny scrub; it is active from morning to night. The whitethroat and the following 11 species all belong to the same genus, which has its main centre of distribution in the Mediterranean area.

Orphean Warbler, *Sylvia hortensis,* 6 in. Breeds in south Europe, north Africa and south-west Asia; occasionally seen in England. It is a shy bird, sheltering in the tree-tops in gardens, orchards and olive groves, and feeding on insects and berries. As the name suggests it is an excellent singer, its voice somewhat resembling that of the blackbird.

Sardinian Warbler, *Sylvia melanocephala,* 5¼ in. Breeds along the whole of the Mediterranean coastline, in thick hedges and bushes. It is easy to distinguish by the red ring round the eye.

Blackcap, *Sylvia atricapilla,* 5½ in. Breeds throughout Europe, except in the far north, as well as in north Africa and west Asia. The female has a rust-brown crown. They live mainly in deciduous woods, parks and gardens and sing well.

Barred Warbler, *Sylvia nisoria,* 6 in. Breeds in east Europe and west Asia, usually in thorn and sloe scrub, hedges and on the edges of woods. When

(above) Whitethroat; Orphean Warbler; Sardinian Warbler
(centre) Blackcap
(below) Barred Warbler; Lesser Whitethroat

singing they first fly up and then glide down with outspread wings.

Lesser Whitethroat, *Sylvia curruca*, 5¼ in. Breeds throughout Europe except in the south-west and far north, as well as in large areas of Asia north of the Himalayas. It is very lively and moves around in bushes and on the edges of woods, orchards and hedges and is common in gardens; it even sings after the sun has gone down. The nest is thin and transparent and is found in low trees and bushes.

Garden Warbler, *Sylvia borin*, 5½ in. Breeds nearly everywhere in Europe, except in the most southerly regions, as well as in west Asia. It lives mostly in deciduous woods with thick undergrowth, in parks and gardens. The nest is loosely woven out of root fibres and fine grass and is sometimes lined with horse hair. The male builds so-called "cocks' nests", which are rather shapeless collections of grass.

Marmora's Warbler, *Sylvia sarda*, 4¾ in. Breeds only in the Balearics, Corsica, Sardinia and Sicily, where it lives mainly in the dense maqui.

Spectacled Warbler, *Sylvia conspicillata*, 5 in. Breeds in the southern parts of Spain, France and Italy. It has a white ring round the eye and lives in dry bushy scrub along the coast.

Subalpine Warbler, *Sylvia cantillans*, 4¾ in. Breeds in Spain, along the Mediterranean coasts and eastwards to Persia. It lives in thickets and low bushes.

Ruppell's Warbler, *Sylvia ruppelli*, 5½ in. Breeds in the countries round the Aegean Sea, where it lives in dry bushy scrub.

Dartford Warbler, *Sylvia undata*, 5 in. Breeds in south England, west France, Portugal, Spain, south Italy and northwest Africa. It lives on heathland or in

(fr. above) Garden Warbler; Marmora's Warbler; Spectacled Warbler; Subalpine Warbler; Ruppell's Warbler; Dartford Warbler

maqui. The tail is proportionately long and constantly held erect.

Cetti's Warbler, *Cettia cetti,* 5½ in. Breeds in south Europe, Africa and large areas of Asia. It is lively but shy and wary and lives among bushes, usually in the neighbourhood of water.

River Warbler, *Locustella fluviatilis,* 5 in. Nests in east Germany and eastwards to the Urals, but is also sometimes seen in west Europe. It lives in thick scrub and woodland, usually near water.

Savi's Warbler, *Locustella luscinoides,* 5½ in. Nests in most of central Europe and Spain, sometimes visiting Britain. It lives among lakeside vegetation and in reed-beds.

Grasshopper Warbler, *Locustella naevia,* 5 in. Breeds throughout the whole of central Europe from Ireland and England and further east to eastern Russia. It lives mostly in willow scrub, thickets and undergrowth. It moves about in the grass like a small mouse and scarcely ever flies. The powerful song is rather like the noise made by a grasshopper, and is most often heard at night.

(from above) Cetti's Warbler; River Warbler; Savi's Warbler; Grasshopper Warbler; Lanceolated Warbler; Rufous Warbler
(to the right) Moustached Warbler; Fan-tailed Warbler

Lanceolated Warbler, *Locustella lanceolata,* 4¾ in. Nests from the Urals through Siberia to Japan and has been recorded a few times in west Europe.

Rufous Warbler, *Agrobates galactotes,* 6 in. Breeds in south Portugal, south Spain, south Balkans and north Africa. It lives in gardens, vineyards, olive groves and mimosa woods and often sits on the top of a bush with the broad tail held up. It has a melodious voice which is not unlike that of the sky lark.

Moustached Warbler, *Lusciniola melanopogon,* 5 in. Nests in the Mediterranean countries and further east to central Asia. It lives in reed-beds and bushes near to water.

Fan-tailed Warbler, *Cisticola juncidis,* 4 in. Nests in south Spain and along the Mediterranean coastline in thick grass and high reeds.

Great Reed Warbler, *Acrocephalus arundinaceus,* 7½ in. Breeds in nearly all of Europe, except in Britain and most of Scandinavia; otherwise it is found in north-west Africa and in Asia as far as west Siberia. The large nest is attached to the stems of reeds and consists of dry stems and reed leaves, and is lined with reed-flowers. It sings throughout the day and night, but mostly at night.

Sedge Warbler, *Acrocephalus schoenobaenus,* 5 in. Breeds over most of Europe and also in much of Asia, and in early summer sings throughout the 24 hours. The nest is built in low bushes or in dry grass near to small lakes.

Aquatic Warbler, *Acrocephalus paludicola,* 5 in. Breeds in north Holland, north Germany and further eastwards to the Urals, as well as in Hungary and Italy. It lives in bushes and reeds near to water.

Marsh Warbler, *Acrocephalus palustris,*

(from above) Great Reed Warbler;
Sedge Warbler; Aquatic Warbler;
Marsh Warbler; Reed Warbler

(from left) Olive-tree Warbler; Olivaceous Warbler; Icterine Warbler

5 in. Breeds in south England, Denmark and central Europe from east France eastwards to the Volga. It lives mostly in dense close willow scrub or in nettle thickets. The nest is fixed to the stems of nettles and other plants and built of straw and pieces of root. This is one of the most melodious singers among the warblers and a very good mimic.

Reed Warbler, *Acrocephalus scirpaceus,* 5 in. Breeds in south and central Europe northwards to England and south Scandinavia and eastwards into Asia as far as Persia; it also occurs in north Africa. The cylindrical nest is fastened to reed stems about 3 ft. from the ground. It is built of reed-flowers and grass and lined with feathers, wool and hair.

Olive-tree Warbler, *Hippolais olivetorum,* 6 in. Breeds in Greece and Turkey and in Asia eastwards to China. It lives in olive-groves and oak woods.

(above) Wood Warbler; Chiffchaff; *(below)* Willow Warbler

(from left) Arctic Warbler; Greenish Warbler; Yellow-browed Warbler

Olivaceous Warbler, *Hippolais pallida,* 5 in. Breeds in south Spain and the Balkans and lives mostly in gardens and fields.

Icterine Warbler, *Hippolais icterina,* 5¼ in. Breeds in Europe from east France to the Urals and into Siberia. It is characteristically a garden bird and lives mostly up in the tree-tops. The nest is built of grass and straw, lined with pieces of root, wool and hair. The song is loud and continuous.

Wood Warbler, *Phylloscopus sibilatrix,* 5 in. Breeds in the greater part of north and central Europe and in west Siberia. It moves around in the tree-tops, most frequently in deciduous woods, and feeds on insects and their larvae, mostly aphids. The nest is always built on the ground.

Chiffchaff, *Phylloscopus collybita,* 4¼ in. Nests over the greater part of Europe, Asia Minor, the Caucasus and west Siberia as far as Lake Baikal. The nest consists of grass, leaves and fern fronds and is usually roofed over, with an entrance at the side.

Willow Warbler, *Phylloscopus trochilus,* 4¼ in. Nests throughout north and central Europe and in summertime is probably the commonest bird in the northern half of Europe. Like most others in this family it is a migratory bird and spends the winter in South Africa. It lives mainly in deciduous woods and is on the hunt for insects throughout the day. It builds its nest on the ground.

Arctic Warbler, *Phylloscopus borealis,* 4¾ in. Breeds from Finmark to Kamtchatka. It lives mostly in the tree-tops, but nests on the ground in the neighbourhood of running water.

(from above) Goldcrest; Firecrest

(from left) Common Tailorbird; Black-chested Prinia; Emu Wren; Black-backed Wren

Greenish Warbler, *Phylloscopus trochiloides,* 4¼ in. Breeds from the east coast of Germany eastwards to eastern Siberia and Manchuria; it is occasionally seen in west Europe.

Yellow-browed Warbler, *Phylloscopus inornatus,* 4 in. Breeds in east Siberia, but in autumn may reach many parts of Europe.

Goldcrest, *Regulus regulus,* 3½ in. Breeds nearly everywhere in north and central Europe and locally in south Europe, as well as in Asia as far as Japan. The female lacks the orange stripe on the yellow forehead. It builds high up in the outermost branches of spruce, where some down-hanging twigs are bound with spider silk to form a basis for the small semicircular mossy nest. Goldcrests and firecrests are often put in a separate family.

Firecrest, *Regulus ignicapillus,* 3½ in. Breeds in central and south Europe, but not in Britain, where it is a winter visitor. Very similar to the goldcrest in habits, and appearance, but has a black stripe through the eye.

Common Tailorbird, *Orthotomus sutorius,* 5 in. One of the best known birds in India, Burma and Ceylon. It is found in nearly every garden, in hedges, plantations and small woods, where it hunts insects. To build a nest it pierces holes in the edge of a pair of leaves with its needle-like beak and sews the leaves together with fibres of plantwool or cobweb to form a small sack, in which it builds a nest of plant fibre and dried grass.

Black-chested Prinia, *Prinia flavicans,* 6 in. Found in thorny scrub areas of South Africa.

Emu Wren, *Stipiturus malachurus,* 6 in. Found in the coastal regions of southern Australia. The erect tail consists of six isolated feathers, resembling those of an emu.

Black-backed Wren, *Malurus melanotus,* 4¼ in. Found in eastern Australia, living usually in pairs or in small flocks.

Babblers

The babblers, Timaliidae, are a family of some 300 species, most of which are found in India and Indonesia, some in Africa and a few in Australia and New Guinea. They are closely related to both the warblers and the thrushes. They are poor fliers with short wings and a close soft plumage, and live in rain forests and thick scrub. They feed on insects and berries and go around in small flocks. Many of them chatter and make loud noises, but some have beautiful voices.

Red-billed Leiothrix, *Leiothrix lutea*, 6 in. Found in the Himalayas and south China. A very gracious, but restless and shy bird that is difficult to observe when in thick scrub. Its very unobtrusive song consists of short powerful thrush notes which are repeated continuously.

New Guinea Log-runner, *Orthonyx novae-guineae*, 6 in. Found in the mountain forests of Australia and New Guinea.

Red-capped Babbler, *Timalia pileata*, 7 in. Found from the Himalayas and south China to Indo-China. It has a chestnut-brown forehead and goes around in pairs in scrub or even on the ground.

White-crested Laughing-thrush, *Garrulax leucolophus*, 12 in. Found from the Himalayas to south China; very numerous in thick forests where it goes around in large flocks. At intervals of a few minutes it breaks into high shrill laughter. It feeds on insects, worms, snails and berries. The open nest is made of bamboo leaves and is built low down.

Pilot Bird, *Pycnoptilus floccosus*, 6½ in. Found in south-eastern Australia, where it lives in mountain forests and thick scrub.

(from above) Red-billed Leiothrix;
New Guinea Log-runner; Red-capped Babbler;
White-crested Laughing-thrush;
Pilot Bird

(from above) Song Thrush; Fieldfare; Mistle Thrush; Ring Ouzel; Blackbird

Thrushes

The thrushes, Turdidae, are a family of more than 300 species, which are found over nearly the whole of the world, except in Antarctica. They feed on insects, worms, snails and berries. The young birds are more or less spotted.

Song Thrush, *Turdus ericetorum,* 9 in. This and the following four species belong among the true thrushes, which consist of about 100 species. It breeds almost everywhere in Europe, except in the southernmost parts, as well as in Asia. It is a migratory bird and spends the winter in west Europe and the Mediterranean countries. The song is clear and melodious, and most of the phrases are repeated two, three or four times. It builds a nest in hedges and bushes, often quite low down. The nest is large and consists externally of moss and dried grass; internally there is always a vast saucer, which is usually made of a hardened mixture of mud and decayed wood.

Fieldfare, *Turdus pilaris,* 10 in. A common breeding bird in Germany, Poland, Scandinavia, Finland, Russia and eastwards into Siberia; it winters throughout nearly the whole of Europe. It lives in fields, hedges and among undergrowth, even during the breeding season, when it nests in colonies.

Mistle Thrush, *Turdus viscivorus,* 10½ in. Breeds almost everywhere in Europe and north-west Africa and in Asia north of the Himalayas to Lake Baikal. The food consists of earth-worms, snails, insects, larvae, berries and seeds. The nest is usually built high up in a tree on the edges of a wood, and is covered externally with leaves and lined with roots and dried grass.

Ring Ouzel, *Turdus torquatus,* 9½ in. Breeds in the mountain regions of Britain, Spain, Scandinavia, the Alps, the Carpathians and large parts of the Balkans, as well as in Asia Minor and further east to the Caspian Sea. It feeds mostly on insects, larvae and berries and nests under bushes and in cliff crevices.

Blackbird, *Turdus merula,* 10 in. Breeds everywhere in Europe, except the far north, in north Africa and in Asia to south China. The female is dark brown with a brown bill; the young birds resemble the female, but are more rufous. Once a shy woodland bird it has in many countries become a half-tame urban bird, which is able to find food throughout the year and has, therefore, become resident in towns. It feeds on earthworms, snails, larvae, insects, fruits and seeds. The melodious song is one of the most beautiful bird sounds. The large nest is made externally of dried grass, twigs and withered leaves, lined with mud and it has an inner layer of dry grass.

Rock Thrush, *Monticola saxatilis,* 7½ in. Breeds in rocky areas in the whole of south Europe northwards to south

(above) Rock Thrush
(below) Blue Rock Thrush

France and Hungary, in north Africa and in Asia as far east as south China. It is a lively but wary bird with a rich and full-toned, but subdued song. The food consists of insects, which are taken

(above) Pied Wheatear; Black Wheatear; *(below)* Wheatear; Black-eared Wheatear

(above) Stonechat; Jerdon's Bush Chat; *(below)* Whinchat; Grey Bush Chat

on the ground or chased in the air. It breeds in cliff crevices and holes in walls or amongst boulders, most often at heights of 3,000-8,000 ft. The female is brownish with dark spots.

Blue Rock Thrush, *Monticola solitarius,* 8 in. Breeds in south Europe, north Africa, the Caucasus and south-west Asia and frequents rocky desert regions and bare mountains. It nests in cracks in cliffs and buildings.

Pied Wheatear, *Oenanthe leucomela,* 5¾ in. Breeds in Rumania and in Asia eastwards to Mongolia, and lives in rocky areas.

Black Wheatear, *Oenanthe leucura,* 7 in. Breeds in the Iberian peninsula, south France, Sardinia and north-west Africa, and lives in rocky deserts. The female is duller and brownish.

Wheatear, *Oenanthe oenanthe,* 5¾ in. One of the relatively few birds which breeds over the whole of Europe, in the greater part of north Asia and in Alaska and Greenland. When on the lookout from a stone, it wags the fanned tail and bobs up and down. It feeds mostly on insects and builds a nest in walls and piles of stones, or in gravel pits, but may also nest in house walls. The female has a red-grey back and appears almost brown, but the root of the tail is white as in the male.

Black-eared Wheatear, *Oenanthe hispanica,* 5¾ in. Breeds in the Mediterranean countries and in south-west Asia, usually in arid stony upland areas.

Stonechat, *Saxicola torquata,* 5 in. Breeds in Britain, central and south Europe, north-west Africa and south-west Asia. Similar in appearance to the whinchat but plumper and nests more frequently on commons and in coastal areas.

Jerdon's Bush Chat, *Saxicola jerdoni,* 6 in. Found in the western parts of south-east Asia, where it lives in grassy areas.

Whinchat, *Saxicola rubetra,* 5 in. Breeds in north and central Europe and in west Asia. Distinguished from the stonechat by the prominent eye-stripe and the less upright stance. It lives mostly in marshes, fields and in open country with bushes, and feeds on insects, spiders and earthworms. The nest is built among grasses on the edges of ditches and embankments and under bushes; it consists of thin grass and root fibres.

Grey Bush Chat, *Saxicola ferrea,* 6 in. Found in the Himalayas, Burma and eastwards to China, living in mountain areas.

Buff-streaked Chat, *Campicoloides bifasciata,* 7 in. Found in south Africa. A lively attractive bird usually seen among rocks in hilly areas.

Cliff Chat, *Thamnolaea cinnamomeiventris,* 6½ in. Found in east Africa, the Congo and Abyssinia on stony ground in hilly areas.

(above) Eastern Bluebird
(below) White-rumped Shama

(above) Buff-streaked Chat
(below) Cliff Chat

Eastern Bluebird, *Sialia sialis,* 7 in. Breeds in southern Canada and eastern U.S.A., westwards to the Rocky Mountains. It lives in thick scrub, gardens and orchards, and feeds on insects, which it often catches in the air and on worms and larvae; in winter it also eats fruits and seeds. It nests in hollow trees and will also use nest-boxes.

White-rumped Shama, *Copsychus malabaricus,* 9½ in. Widespread in India, Ceylon, south-east Asia and Indonesia. It lives in bamboo thickets and catches insects on the ground. The song is heard throughout the year and is one of the most melodious of all bird songs.

Redstart, *Phoenicurus phoenicurus,* 5½ in. Breeds almost everywhere in Europe and

(from above) Redstart; Black Redstart;
White-spotted Bluethroat;
Red-spotted Bluethroat
Robin; <u>Magpie Robin</u>

also in north Africa and west Asia to Lake Baikal. It lives mostly in open woods, parks and gardens. The redstart is a restless bird but a pleasant singer. The nest is built in holes in trees or in wood piles but it will also breed in nest-boxes. The female is grey-brown above, buffish below.

Black Redstart, *Phoenicurus ochrurus,* 5½ in. Breeds throughout Europe from south England, Denmark and south Sweden southwards, as well as in west Asia. It is often seen in the neighbourhood of buildings, harbours and railways, where it feeds on insects and larvae. The nest is built in cliff crevices, holes in walls, cellars and out-houses. The female is greyish-brown with a rufous tail.

Red-spotted Bluethroat, *Luscinia suecica suecica,* 5½ in. Breeds in northern Scandinavia, Finland, and north Russia in the tundra regions of Siberia. It lives mostly in willow scrub and mossy terrain and builds close to the ground among vegetation. In spring the male has a bright blue throat with a red-brown spot in the middle. In autumn the throat is almost white. The female has a whitish throat edged with black.

White-spotted Bluethroat, *Luscinia suecica cyanecula,* 5½ in. This race of the bluethroat breeds in central Europe from France and Holland to west Russia. It lives mostly in damp scrub and among reeds.

Robin, *Erithacus rubecula,* 5½ in. Breeds nearly everywhere in Europe as well as in north Africa and west Asia. Essentially a woodland bird, it is also found in parks and gardens and shows great trust in man. It feeds mostly on insects and larvae, but also takes berries and other plant food.

<u>Magpie</u> Robin, *Copsychus saularis,* 7 in. Found in India and south-east Asia, and very common in gardens where it hunts insects among the bushes and eats berries. In its home country it is reckoned as one of the best singers.

Nightingale, *Luscinia megarhynchos,* 6½ in. Breeds in England, central and south Europe, north Africa and Asia Minor. Very similar to the next species but the tail is more red-brown. The song is rich and musical and remarkably persistent, often going on throughout the night.

Thrush Nightingale, *Luscinia luscinia,* 6½ in. An inconspicuously coloured bird, which is found from south Scandinavia, south Finland, Poland and Rumania eastwards to Siberia. It lives hidden in damp scrub and sings only for a month, although during this period it sings throughout the 24 hours. The song consists of a series of melodious notes, which alternate with hoarse bubbling sounds. It feeds on insects, larvae, worms and snails, and builds a nest on the ground under bushes; the eggs are either coffee-brown or dark green. The nest saucer is deep, and along the edge of it there is a fringe of dry leaves, usually of oak. It is a migratory bird and winters in tropical East Africa.

Black-backed Forktail, *Enicurus immaculatus,* 11 in. Found in India and parts of

(from left) Nightingale; Thrush Nightingale

south-east Asia. The long cleft tail, which it wags up and down, makes up over half the body length. It feeds on mountain slopes where it moves around among the stones like a wagtail and catches small invertebrates.

Spotted Forktail, *Enicurus maculatus,* 11 in. Very similar to the last species, but spotted on the back and with a black breast.

(from left) Black-backed Forktail; Spotted Forktail

Mockingbird

can imitate 20 to 30 other bird songs, as well as the creak of a door, the scratch of a gramophone needle, the brakes of a car or a factory hooter, to mention just a few examples.

Brown Thrasher, *Toxostoma rufum*, 10½ in. Found in south-east Canada and eastern United States, living in thick undergrowth, where it hunts for insects on the ground, but also takes fruit. It often sits in the bushes and wags its tail restlessly. It defends its nest by attacking intruders and cackling.

Catbird, *Dumetella carolinensis*, 9 in. Found in southern Canada and eastern United States, to the Rocky Mountains. It resembles the wrens in form and in its restless behaviour. It feeds on insects and berries. It sings well but its alarm note is like the mewing of a kitten.

Mockingbirds

The mockingbirds, Mimidae, are a family of some 30 species, which are found only in America, mostly in Mexico. They are related both to the thrushes and the wrens. The majority live in forests, usually low down in the undergrowth or even on the forest floor. Most of them are remarkable singers and many have an exceptional capacity for imitating other voices and sounds.

Mockingbird, *Mimus polyglottos*, 10 in. Widespread over the eastern and southern United States, living in parks and gardens and even nesting in the neighbourhood of man. The relatively large nest is made of twigs, grass and root fibres and built in a tree. The male helps with the nest building and also with the incubation of the eggs and the feeding of the young. This is the best of all bird mimics; some

(above) Brown Thrasher
(below) Catbird

Wrens

The wrens, Troglodytidae, form a family of some 60 species, which are closely related to the thrushes. They are American birds, and only one species has spread to Europe and Asia. They build large spherical nests with a side entrance, and in many species the family keeps together for such a long period that the young from the first clutch may help the parents to feed those from the second clutch. In contrast to most other birds both males and females sing, and they do this the whole year round, even when the weather is cold and damp.

Wren, *Troglodytes troglodytes,* 3¾ in. Widespread over the whole of Europe, except in northernmost Scandinavia, as well as in north Asia, Canada and U.S.A. The small short tail is almost always held erect, and the song is surprisingly loud for such a small bird. The wren is common in woods and parks, where it builds a nest in the fork of a tree, between tree roots or in bushes. The nest is spherical with an entrance at the side, built of leaves, grass, moss and twigs, and lined with hair, wool and feathers. The main structure of the nest is built by the cock, who may make several, but only one is used for breeding and this one is lined by the hen.

Bewick's Wren, *Thryomanes bewicki,* 4¾ in. Found nearly everywhere in North Africa. A very lively bird, which builds a nest similar to that of the wren; it may also breed in nest-boxes.

Fulvous-naped Marsh-wren, *Campylorhynchus nuchalis,* 7 in. Found in South America.

(at right, from above) Wren; Bewick's Wren; Fulvous-naped Marsh-wren

Dippers

The dippers, Cinclidae, are a small family of 5 species, found in Europe, Asia north of the Himalayas to China, western North America and Mexico and further southwards to Argentina. They resemble the large wrens, to which they are related. The plumage is close and smooth with a thick layer of down and the eyebrows are feather-clad. They have powerful legs, short strong beaks and short tails, which are often held erect. The different species are all rather similar, and the sexes are alike. The plumage of the young birds is spotted. The dippers are the only passerines that can swim and dive.

Dipper, *Cinclus cinclus,* 7 in. Breeds in most parts of Europe and extends into Asia. It usually lives in the neighbour-

(from above) Dipper; American Dipper

over the greater part of the earth. The family consists of two groups, the wagtails, which are mottled in black and white or yellow, and which have a long tail which is continuously wagged up and down, and the pipits, which resemble larks and are brownish with longitudinal stripes and shorter tails.

Yellow-headed Wagtail, *Motacilla citreola*, 7 in. Found on the tundras of east Russia and Siberia. The male in summer plumage is canary yellow on the head, neck and belly and has a grey-black back; in winter he is grey-brown on the back like the female.

Grey Wagtail, *Motacilla cinerea*, 7 in. Breeds in central and south Europe, including Britain, and in north and central Asia to Kamtchatka and Japan. It lives near running water in hilly country and also near sewage farms, and feeds on insects and small aquatic animals. The large coarse nest is usually built in the neighbourhood of water between stones, in holes in walls or under bridges. In summer the male has a black throat stripe, which is lacking in his winter dress and in the females.

White Wagtail, *Motacilla alba alba*, 7 in. One of the few bird species which is found over the whole of Europe, in north Africa and in Asia north of the Himalayas eastwards to south China, usually on cultivated land, along the edges of lakes and on the sea coast. It is on the move looking for insects from early morning to late in the evening with only a few rests. It feeds mostly on midges, flies and small beetles, which it often seizes in the air; it also eats seeds. Scarcely any other bird builds its nest in such a variety of places—on the roofs of houses, in wood piles, tree holes, stone walls, in wharfs and plough furrows; there are even records of it build-

hood of rivers and waterfalls, and there are records of it building its spherical nest on the cliff wall behind a waterfall, so that it had to fly through the downpour of water. It dives from a stone on the edge of a lake or out in the river, and runs round on the bottom with half spread wings for several seconds, feeding on mayfly and other aquatic larvae. A moment after it comes up it will dive again and can repeat this process time and time again. It often stands on a stone and nods with its head, wags its tail and sings its short twittering song.

American Dipper, *Cinclus mexicanus*, 7¼ in. Found from Alaska to Panama, in mountain regions in the neighbourhood of rivers and waterfalls.

Wagtails and Pipits

The wagtails and pipits, Motacillidae, are a well-defined family of about 50 species of insect-eating birds, distributed

(from above) Yellow-headed Wagtail; Grey Wagtail
(front) White Wagtail; Pied Wagtail

ing in a fishing boat which was in use. The female has less black on the head and breast than the male, and in winter both sexes have a white throat with a black crescentic throat patch.

Pied Wagtail, *Motacilla alba yarrelli.* This is a subspecies of the last species and occurs in Britain. In summer the back is black in the male, greyer in the female.

Blue-headed Yellow Wagtail, *Mota-*

cilla flava flava, 6½ in. Found in Europe and west Siberia. It feeds on small insects, usually in damp places, and builds a nest on the ground.

Grey-headed Wagtail, *Motacilla flava thunbergi.* This and the following two are races of the last species. The present one is found in Norway, Sweden and Finland and has a dark grey head.

Black-headed Wagtail, *Motacilla flava feldegg.* Found in the Balkans. In summer

(from left) Blue-headed Yellow Wagtail; Grey-headed Wagtail;
Black-headed Wagtail; Yellow Wagtail

(from above) Tree Pipit; Meadow Pipit

the male has a black forehead and cheeks.

Yellow Wagtail, *Motacilla flava flavissima.* Breeds in Britain and neighbouring parts of Europe. The head is yellow and olive-green.

Tree Pipit, *Anthus trivialis,* 6 in. This and the following 7 species belong among the pipits, which have a very wide distribution over practically the whole of the globe. The tree pipit breeds in the greater part of Europe and west Asia, and lives in both deciduous and coniferous forests. It hunts for insects and larvae on the ground, and only sings in flight. The nest is built in a sheltered place on the edges of ditches or under bushes.

Meadow Pipit, *Anthus pratensis,* 5¾ in. Breeds in north and central Europe and in the western part of Siberia. It lives in fields, marshes, dunes and on heathland, where it runs around on the ground looking for worms, insects and seeds. It sings in the air and glides down singing to its starting point. The nest is completely sheltered in a grass tuft and is built of dried grass.

Tawny Pipit, *Anthus campestris,* 6½ in. Breeds in south and central Europe, northwards to Denmark and south Sweden, as well as in north Africa and west Asia. It lives mostly in sandy places with sparse vegetation and feeds almost exclusively on insects, larvae and snails. The nest is built on the ground and lined with grass.

(above) Tawny Pipit; Red-throated Pipit
(below) Richard's Pipit; Rock Pipit

(above) Pink-throated Longclaw
(below) Australian Pipit

Red-throated Pipit, *Anthus cervinus,*
5¾ in. Breeds on the tundras and moorland heaths from northernmost Lapland
eastwards to Kamtchatka. On its migrations to its winter quarters in north
Africa it is often observed in Europe.

Richard's Pipit, *Anthus novaeseelandiae,*
7 in. Widespread in Asia, migrating
westwards and sometimes seen in Britain.
It lives in grassy areas and rice plantations.

Rock Pipit, *Anthus spinoletta,* 6½ in.
Breeds mainly on skerries and cliffs along
the coasts of Europe and north Asia,
feeds on insects and small animals from
the shore, and builds a nest in cliff
crevices or under large boulders. The
very similar water pipit breeds in the
mountain areas of Europe.

Pink-throated Longclaw, *Macronyx
ameliae,* 7¾ in. Found along the east coast
of South Africa.

Australian Pipit, *Anthus australis,* 6½ in.
Widespread in Tasmania and Australia,
where it lives either singly or in pairs on
open land.

Bulbuls and Leafbirds

The bulbuls and leafbirds are found
widely distributed over Africa, Madagascar and tropical Asia, and are very
common within their range. They are
thrushlike birds, many of which have
long hair-like feathers on the nape and
back.

Fairy Bluebird, *Irena puella,* 9½ in.
Found in small flocks in the rain forests
of India, south-east Asia and Indonesia.
It feeds on fruits and insects. The female
is duller in colour than the male.

(above) Fairy Bluebird
(centre) Red-whiskered Bulbul
(below) Black Bulbul

69

Red-whiskered Bulbul, *Pycnonotus joco-sus,* 7½ in. Common in many parts of India, south-east Asia and China, where it lives in woods, parks and gardens. The red ear patches of the female are smaller than those of the male, and the female herself is also somewhat smaller.

Black Bulbul, *Microscelis madagascariensis,* 10 in. Found in mountain regions in Africa and south Asia. It lives in the tree-tops and feeds on insects and fruits.

Golden-fronted Leafbird, *Chloropsis aurifrons,* 7½ in. Found in India, south-east Asia and Ceylon. A very lively bird, which lives high up in the tree-tops, in pairs during the breeding season and in small flocks during the rest of the year. Its song consists of deep fluty tones and it also mimics other bird calls.

Common Iora, *Aegithina tiphia,* 5½ in. Very common in India in gardens and on the outskirts of villages. The song of the male is pretty and melodious. Unlike the male, the female is almost yellow-green.

(above) White-bellied Cuckoo-shrike
(below) Black Cuckoo-shrike

(above) Golden-fronted Leafbird
(below) Common Iora

Wood Shrikes and Minivets

This family, the Campephagidae, has some 80 species, found from Africa south of the Sahara over south Asia to Australia, Tasmania and the South Sea Islands. The birds vary in size from a sparrow to a jackdaw, and most have shrike-like bills with a hooked point and bristles at the root. The plumage is close, and on the upper rump the feathers have a thick stiff shaft which narrows and becomes thin at the tip; these feathers are so loosely fixed into the thin skin that they easily fall out. They almost all live in the rain forests in pairs during the breeding season and in small flocks during the rest of the year. They feed on larvae, but may also catch insects in the

(above) Black Caterpillar-catcher
(below) Orange Minivet

air in the manner of flycatchers; many also eat berries and other fruits. The plumage is very variable between the two sexes.

White-bellied Cuckoo-shrike, *Coracina hypoleuca*, 10 in. Found in north Australia, New Guinea and the Solomons. It lives in open woods and goes about either in pairs or small flocks.

Black Cuckoo-shrike, *Campephaga sulphurata*, 8¼ in. Found in east and south Africa, where it lives in the forests.

Black Caterpillar-catcher, *Edolisoma melas*, 9½ in. Found in the forests of New Guinea.

Orange Minivet, *Pericrocotus flammeus*, 9 in. Found in India and Ceylon, living in the tree-tops in rain forests, from sea level up to heights of 6,000 ft. The female is dark grey and matt yellow.

Swallows

The swallows, Hirundinidae, are a well-defined family of some 75 species which are found almost everywhere, except in the polar regions and New Zealand. They are wonderful fliers and feed on insects which they take in the air over open land or over lakes and deserts; they can also drink without touching the ground. Most swallows live in the neighbourhood of man and usually plaster their nests of mud on to houses.

Swallow, *Hirundo rustica,* 7½ in. Breeds in Europe, north Africa, Asia and north America and many spend the winter in south Africa. They are recognisable by the cleft tail with the two very long outer feathers. In good weather swallows fly high up, but when the barometer is low and insects are nearer to the ground the swallows also fly low. The saucer-formed nest is made of mud mixed with spit and lined with feathers and wool. It is most often fixed on to beams in barns, stables and lofts.

(from left) Swallow; Red-rumped Swallow

House Martin

nest is usually built in caves and cliff holes and has an entrance tunnel.

House Martin, *Delichon urbica,* 5 in. Breeds over the whole of Europe, in north Africa and in most of Asia to Japan and China. The feet are completely feathered. The spherical mud nest usually has a small entrance hole at the top; it is placed on steep cliffs, rock faces and house walls.

Sand Martin, *Riparia riparia,* 4¾ in. Breeds over the whole of Europe, in north Africa, north America and north Asia. It builds in colonies in the upper parts of gravel pits and sandy slopes, and uses its sharp claws to dig a perpendicular nest hole into the cliff; the nest is lined with grass and feathers.

Red-rumped Swallow, *Hirundo daurica,* 7 in. Breeds in south Spain, the Balkans, north Africa and large parts of Asia. The

Cliff Swallow, *Petrochelidon pyrrhonota,* 6 in. Breeds in North America and winters in South America. It nests in large colonies and originally built its

(from left) Sand Martin; Cliff Swallow; Nyasa Rock-martin; Purple Martin

Larks

The larks, Alaudidae, are a well-defined family of about 80 species; the majority are found in Africa, the remainder in Europe and Asia, apart from two species in Australia and one in America. The hind claw is long and straight. Larks live in fields and meadows, deserts and steppes, and feed on insects and other small animals, and in winter on seeds. They build their nests on the ground.

Wood Lark, *Lululla arborea*, 6 in. Breeds everywhere in Europe except Ireland, Scotland, north Scandinavia and north Finland, as well as in north Africa and Asia. It usually lives where woods and heathland meet, and feeds on insects, worms and seeds.

Sky Lark, *Alauda arvensis*, 7 in. Breeds throughout Europe, north Africa and parts of Asia; the European larks winter in west Europe and north Africa. Sky

(above) Rufous-chested Swallow
(below) Black and White Swallow

pitcher-formed mud-nest on cliffs, but now usually builds under eaves.

Nyasa Rock-martin, *Ptyonoprogne rufigula*, 5 in. Found from east Africa south to Mashonaland. During savanna fires it flies out to catch the insects which are disturbed by the flames.

Purple Martin, *Progne subis*, 7½ in. Breeds in America from south Canada to Mexico and winters in south America. It originally built in colonies in hollow trees, but now nests also in nest-boxes. The female does not have the iridescence of the male and is more brownish.

Rufous-chested Swallow, *Hirundo semirufa*, 7½ in. Found in tropical Africa from Senegal to Kenya.

Black and White Swallow, *Cheramoeca leucosternum*, 7 in. Found over the whole of Australia, where it goes about in small flocks over open land.

(from above) Wood Lark; Sky Lark

(from left) Shore Lark; Crested Lark

Breeds in parts of north Scandinavia and also in the upland regions of north Africa, north and central Asia and north and central America. It winters in more low-lying country, often near the sea-shore.

Crested Lark, *Galerida cristata,* 6¾ in. Breeds in Europe from Denmark and south Sweden southwards (but not in Britain), as well as in north Africa and large parts of Asia. It is a resident bird and lives amongst other places along roads and near railway installations, farms and gardens. It moves about quickly, looking for insects, larvae, seeds and buds. The nest is built on the edge of a grass tuft or in refuse dumps.

Calandra Lark, *Melanocorypha calandra,* 7½ in. Breeds in south Europe, north Africa and west Asia; occasionally seen in central and north Europe. It lives in open fields and plains. The song is like that of the sky lark but louder.

Black Lark, *Melanocorypha yeltoniensis,* 7½ in. Breeds in south-east Russia and central Asia, but sometimes strays to

larks feed on insects and seeds and the nest is built in a hollow in the grass. Like other larks they nearly always sing high up in the air with whirring wings. They have been introduced into Australia and New Zealand and some places in America.

Shore Lark, *Eremophila alpestris,* 6½ in.

(from left) Calandra Lark; Black Lark; Lesser Short-toed Lark; Short-toed Lark

(*above*) Cape Clapper Lark; Dusky Lark
(*below*) Chestnut-backed Sparrow-lark; Hoopoe-lark

west Europe. The female is light brown, as is the male in autumn plumage.

Lesser Short-toed Lark, *Calandrella rufescens,* 5½ in. Breeds in fields and desert areas in south Spain, north Africa and Asia Minor.

Short-toed Lark, *Calandrella brachydactyla,* 5½ in. Breeds in south Europe, north Africa, central and south Asia. It lives mostly in sandy wastes and steppes, but may also occur in cultivated regions.

Cape Clapper Lark, *Mirafra apiata,* 6¼ in. Found in south Africa.

Dusky Lark, *Mirafra nigricans,* 7½ in. Found in south Africa, on bushy savanna.

Chestnut-backed Sparrow-lark, *Eremopterix leucotis,* 5 in. Found in tropical Africa, on sandy and stony areas, and may sometimes raid cornfields in large flocks.

Hoopoe-lark, *Alaemon alaudipes,* 8¾ in. Found in north-east Africa and southwest Arabia. It is a desert bird and a fast runner.

Ganges Sand Lark, *Calandrella raytal,* 5 in. Found in north India and Burma.

Rufous-winged Bush Lark, *Mirafra assamica,* 6 in. Found in India, Ceylon, Burma and Siam.

(*above*) Ganges Sand Lark
(*below*) Rufous-winged Bush Lark

75

Noisy Scrub-bird

Scrub-birds

The scrub-birds, Atrichornithidae, are an Australasian family of two species, which, in spite of their appearance and size are related to the lyrebirds. They resemble wrens with a long tail and run about in thick undergrowth after insects, worms and snails, but do not fly. The nest is roofed, with a side entrance.

Noisy Scrub-bird, *Atrichornis clamosa*, 8½ in. Once very common in thick forest in west Australia. Its fluty song ended in a noisy croaking.

Lyrebirds

The lyrebirds, Menuridae, consist of only two or three species; they are the largest of the passerines. The tail of the female consists of 12 long almost identical feathers, that of the male has 16 feathers, of which the outermost and largest are curved, the central ones very narrow and the remainder long and downy. Lyrebirds live in the forests of south-east Australia and feed on insects, worms, snails and seeds. They mostly use the wings when running but seldom fly. The male builds mounds of earth on which to display. He lifts and spreads the tail, lays it forwards over the back and at the same time gives forth a cascade of melodious notes. The large nest is built low down or right on the ground by the female which also incubates the single egg and rears the young.

Northern Lyrebird, *Menura alberti*. Somewhat smaller than the next species.

Lyrebird, *Menura novaehollandiae*, 37 in., of which the tail accounts for 22½ in. The grey-brown female is 31 in., with a tail 17 in.

(from left) Northern Lyrebird; Lyrebird

(above) White-barred Bush-shrike
(centre) Chestnut-crowned Ant-thrush
(below) Boddaert's Ant-thrush

Ant-catchers

The ant-catchers, Formicariidae, are a central and south American family with a number of species ranging in size from a rook to nearly as small as a humming-bird. Some species follow wandering ants, to take the insects they bring.

White-barred Bush-shrike, *Thamnophilus doliatus*, 6 in. Found in open woodland in northern South America.

Chestnut-crowned Ant-thrush, *Grallaria ruficapilla*, 7¾ in. Almost tailless. The voice consists of three powerful notes.

Boddaert's Ant-thrush, *Formicarius colma*, 7 in. Lives on the ground and does not fly.

Wood-hewer

The wood-hewers, Dendrocolaptidae, consist of about 50 species, found from south Mexico to Argentina. The majority have long sickle-shaped bills and stiff tail feathers. Like the woodpeckers and tree-creepers they climb in a spiral up the stems of trees searching for spiders, insects and larvae. They breed in tree holes.

Red-billed Wood-hewer, *Campylorhamphus trochilirostris*, 9¾ in. Found in northern South America.

Oven-birds

The oven-birds, Furnariidae, from central and south America consist of over 200 species, closely related to the last

(above) Red-billed Wood-hewer
(below) Azara's Firewood-gatherer

Red Oven-bird

Rifleman, *Acanthisitta chloris,* 3 in. Lives in open woods and climbs up the stems of trees like a tree creeper, looking for insects and spiders. It usually builds its spherical nest in a tree hole.

Pittas

The pittas, Pittidae, are a family of about 23 brightly coloured thrush-sized birds with long legs and short tails. They have their main centre of distribution in Indonesia, but extend to India, China, Japan, New Guinea and north Australia, and there are two species in Africa. They are shy birds, which go around on the ground in thick rain forests. They seldom use the wings and if they do they only fly for short distances. They feed on insects, worms and small snails, which they kill by shaking against the ground.

family. They live mostly on insects and are usually brownish, but are variable in appearance and habits; some resemble larks, some thrushes and others tree-creepers.

Azara's Firewood-gatherer, *Anumbius anumbi,* 7¾ in. Builds a large nest of twigs, which it brings cross-ways in the bill; it loses so many of these during building operations that a whole pile of twigs accumulates under the nest. The entrance is above and a spiral tunnel leads down into the nest chamber.

Red Oven-bird, *Furnarius rufus,* 7¼ in. Found in open country, where it builds a dome-shaped nest of mud on a horizontal branch; the nest chamber is lined with dried grass and feathers. The nest weighs 8-10 lb. and is used for several years.

New Zealand Wrens

The New Zealand wrens, Acanthisittidae, consist of only 4 small birds with short tails, restricted to New Zealand, where they live in trees and feed on insects.

(above) Rifleman
(below) Angola Pitta; Black-headed Pitta

Angola Pitta, *Pitta angolensis,* 7 in. Found from Angola to Liberia and Sierra Leone. The food consists principally of termites. The pear-shaped nest has a long entrance tunnel and is built in thorny trees.

Black-headed Pitta, *Pitta novae-guineae,* 7 in. Lives in the forests of New Guinea.

Tyrant Flycatchers

The tyrant flycatchers, Tyrannidae, are the largest purely American bird family and contain about 400 species, which live mostly in woods, parks and gardens. They fly well and catch insects in the air. They are very bold and will attack and fight both crows and birds of prey, which they circle round or strike on the back with the beak.

Scissor-tailed Flycatcher, *Muscivora forficata,* 15½ in. Breeds in the United States from Kansas to south Texas, and winters in central America.

Eastern Kingbird, *Tyrannus tyrannus,* 7¾ in. Breeds from central Canada to Florida, and winters in South America. Known for its aggressive behaviour towards larger birds.

Vermilion Flycatcher, *Pyrocephalus rubinus,* 6 in. Found in America from Texas to Argentina. The female is less red and more brown than the male.

Kiskadee Flycatcher, *Pitangus sulphuratus,* 9¾ in. Found from Texas to Argentina. It lives mostly on flying insects and fruit, but may also catch small fish, like a kingfisher.

Royal Great-crest, *Onychorhynchus coronatus,* 6¼ in. Found from Mexico to northern South America. The male can raise his conspicuous red crest like a feather brush.

(from above) Scissor-tailed Flycatcher; Eastern Kingbird; Vermilion Flycatcher; Kiskadee Flycatcher; Royal Great-crest

(above) Golden-headed Manakin
(below) Blue-backed Manakin

Manakins

The manakins, Pipridae, are a family of some 60 species of small birds with short bills, found from south Mexico to Argentina. The name originates from the Dutch manneken, a little man. In habits they resemble the tits and live in pairs or in small flocks in forests, where they feed on insects and berries. The male clears display areas by removing leaves and twigs and attracts the females by singing and producing sounds with the help of special wing feathers. The male is polygamous and leaves the female after mating and helps neither in nest-building, incubation, nor rearing the young.

Golden-headed Manakin, *Pipra erythrocephala,* 3½ in.

Blue-backed Manakin, *Chiroxiphia pareola,* 3½ in. Two males sing in front of a female on the display arena; exceptionally up to 5 males may take part in this concert.

Chatterers

The chatterers, Cotingidae, are an American family of about 90 species, found from Mexico to Argentina. They vary considerably in appearance, behaviour and size; the largest are as large as ravens, the smallest as small as wrens. They are all fruit-eaters, but many also eat snails and insects and some take lizards and other small animals. Some screech and croak, others make clock-like notes.

Naked-throated Bell-bird, *Procnias nudicollis,* 10 in. Found in the rain forests of south-east Brazil. In the female, which is green above and yellow below, the naked throat is black. The call of the male resembles the noise of a hammer hitting a metal plate.

Pompadour Chatterer, *Xipholena punicea,* 7¼ in. Found in the rain forests of

(above) Naked-throated Bell-bird;
Pompadour Chatterer
(below) Banded Chatterer

(above) Umbrella Bird
(below) Cock-of-the-rock;
Peruvian Cock-of-the-rock

Venezuela, Guiana and the Amazon, where it lives in tree-tops. The male is purple with white wings, the female grey.

Banded Chatterer, *Cotinga cincta,* 7 in. Found in the forest-clad coastal areas of south-east Brazil. The female is mainly grey-brown. They may be found in large flocks and are shot in great numbers for their flesh and feathers.

Umbrella Bird, *Cephalopterus ornatus,* 19 in. Found in the northern parts of South America from Ecuador to the Amazon in Brazil. On the forehead there is a big feather mop which can be erected, and a 10-inch-long feather-clad skin fold hangs down from the neck. Their powerful screech sounds at a distance

like the roar of a bull. They feed on fruits and insects.

Cock-of-the-rock, *Rupicola rupicola,* 15 in. Found in the mountain regions of Venezuela, Guiana and north Brazil. The crest on the head is always erect; the female is brown and has a smaller crest. Unlike other chatterers this species has a courtship display in which several males and females dance on a previously cleared area of the forest floor.

Peruvian Cock-of-the-rock, *Rupicola peruviana,* 15 in. Found in the north-west of South America; one form has orange plumage.

Plant-cutters

The plant-cutters, Phytotomidae, are a small family of three or four species from the south of South America. They are finch-like birds with short, powerful bills which have a saw-like edge. They cut leaves, buds and fruit from trees and can sometimes do damage. They fly awkwardly.

Chilean Plant-cutter, *Phytotoma rara,* 7 in. Found in central Chile. The female is paler and greyish.

Chilean Plant-cutter

Woodpeckers

THE WOODPECKERS and related birds, the Piciformes, are mainly found in the tropics of Africa, Asia and America, although some occur in temperate and northern regions. They live in woodland and have climbing feet with two toes facing forward and two backwards. They feed on insects or fruit and lay their white eggs in tree holes or even in holes in the ground. The group contains the toucans, honey-guides, barbets, true woodpeckers, jacamars and puff-birds.

Banded Broadbill; Long-tailed Broadbill

Broadbills

The broadbills, Eurylaemidae, are a family of about 20 species mostly found in India, south-east Asia, with a few in Africa. They are plump birds with flattened hooked beaks, which are very broad at the root. They live in forests and feed on insects and fruit. The long nest with a side entrance hangs down from a thin branch.

Banded Broadbill, *Eurylaimus javanicus*, 9 in. Found in Malaya and Burma. It often lives in woods along rivers.

Long-tailed Broadbill, *Psarisomus dalhousiae*, 10 in. Found in India and south-east Asia.

Toucans

The toucans, Rhamphastidae, form a group of lively and noisy birds with about 37 species. They live in the forests from Mexico to Argentina and are particularly numerous in the rain forests of the Amazon. The plumage is very variegated, but the main characteristic is the exceptionally large bill, which is saw-like at the edge. In spite of its size this bill is light in weight, as there are air spaces between the thin bony walls of which it is built. The very long tongue is narrow and flat and fringed with fine horny threads, so that it resembles a feather. The toucans live mostly on tree fruits, but also take some larger insects and smaller reptiles, as well as the eggs and young of small birds. They lay eggs in tree holes.

Toco Toucan, *Rhamphastos toco*, 22 in. Found in high-lying areas from Guiana through Brazil to Paraguay.

Sulphur-breasted Toucan, *Rhamphastos piscivorus*, 21 in. Found from South Mexico to Honduras and often regarded as a race of the last species.

(above) Toco Toucan; Sulphur-breasted Toucan
(below) Red-breasted Toucan; Swainson's Doubtful Toucan; Ariel Toucan; Red-billed Toucan

Red-breasted Toucan, *Rhamphastos dicolorus,* 19 in. Found in south-eastern Brazil and Paraguay.

Swainson's Doubtful Toucan, *Rhamphastos swainsoni,* 23 in.

Ariel Toucan, *Rhamphastos ariel,* 17½ in. Widely distributed in the coastal forests of Brazil.

Red-billed Toucan, *Rhamphastos tucanus,* 21 in. Found in Guiana and north Brazil.

Baillon's Aracari, *Andigena bailloni,* 15 in. Found in south-east Brazil.

Black-necked Aracari, *Pteroglossus aracari,* 17 in. Found in the forests of eastern Brazil.

Spot-billed Toucanet, *Selenidera maculirostris,* 13 in. Smaller than the other toucans and with a shorter bill and tail.

(from above) Baillon's Aracari; Black-necked Aracari; Spot-billed Toucanet

(from above) Lesser Honey-guide; Black-throated Honey-guide; Malay Honey-guide

that there is a bee nest nearby. The natives break open the nest to remove the beeswax and give the bird a fitting portion of the booty.

Malay Honey-guide, *Indicator archipelagus,* 6½ in. Found in the forests of Malaya, Sumatra and Borneo.

Barbets

The barbets, Capitonidae, consist of about 76 species varying in size from a wren to a shrike. The majority are found in Africa, but there are also many in the Indian region and in South America. They live mostly on the edges of forests and on savannas with sparse tree growth. The food consists mainly of fruits but they also take many insects and exceptionally small lizards and birds'

Honey-guides and Honey-birds

This family, the Indicatoridae, consists of about 13 species of at the most starling-sized birds. They are inconspicuously coloured, and the majority are found in Africa. Their tough skin is a good protection against insect stings. They lay their eggs in other birds' nests.

Lesser Honey-guide, *Indicator minor,* 5½ in. Found in bushy savanna in east Africa.

Black-throated Honey-guide, *Indicator indicator,* 7 in. Found in almost the whole of Africa south of the Sahara and is the commonest of the honey-guides. It feeds on bees, bee larvae and beeswax, a diet that almost no other animal can digest. The natives follow its call out in the forest, when it is hopping from tree to tree. When it sits still this is the sign

(above) Golden-rumped Tinker-bird
(centre) Levaillant's Barbet
(below) Black-collared Barbet

(from above) Great Barbet; Lineated Barbet;
Indian Blue-throated Barbet

Woodpeckers

The woodpeckers, Picidae, consist of over 200 species varying in size from a sparrow to a jackdaw and living in wooded regions over most of the world, except in Australasia and Madagascar. Most have a powerful straight bill, which ends in a chisel-formed edge. The small sticky tongue has backward-directed horny spines and can be pushed far out of the mouth; it is used for catching larvae and insects. The woodpeckers do some damage by eating cone-seeds and hacking holes in tree bark, but on balance are probably beneficial because they eat many injurious insects and larvae.

Woodpeckers climb tree trunks in a wide spiral, using the short stiff tail feathers as props. Their voice is usually a sharp screech, and particularly during the breeding season the males of many

eggs. They usually make a nest in a rotten tree or in a bank.

Golden-rumped Tinker-bird, *Pogoniulus bilineatus*, 7¼ in. Found in east and south-east Africa.

Levaillant's Barbet, *Trachyphonus vaillanti*, 7¾ in. Found in Angola, Tanganyika, Rhodesia and eastern South Africa.

Black-collared Barbet, *Lybius torquatus*, 7¼ in. Found over most of southern Africa.

Great Barbet, *Megalaima virens*, 11½ in. Found in northern India and eastwards to Burma and China.

Lineated Barbet, *Megalaima zeylanica*, 11 in. Found in India and Ceylon.

Indian Blue-throated Barbet, *Megalaima asiatica*, 9 in. Found in India and south-east Asia.

(from left) Great Spotted Woodpecker;
Lesser-spotted Woodpecker;
Middle-spotted Woodpecker

species produce a drumming note by hammering very rapidly with the beak against dead wood.

The family can be divided into two subfamilies: the true woodpeckers, which are resident birds, and the wrynecks, which are migratory.

Great Spotted Woodpecker, *Dendrocopus major,* 9 in. Breeds over most of Europe, north and central Asia and north-west Africa and feeds mainly on insects, larvae and cone seeds. Like the majority of the woodpeckers it chisels its nest out of a tree trunk; a circular hole leads into a large chamber in the wood, within which the white eggs are laid on a layer of soft wood chips.

Lesser Spotted Woodpecker, *Dendrocopus minor,* 5¾ in. Breeds in nearly the whole of Europe, in north Asia and in north-west Africa. It feeds almost exclusively on insects and larvae. The crown of the female is whitish or yellowish.

Middle Spotted Woodpecker, *Dendrocopus medius,* 8½ in. Found in most of central and south Europe and west Asia.

Three-toed Woodpecker, *Picoides tridactylus,* 8¾ in. Breeds in Scandinavia and further eastwards to eastern Asia, as well as in certain regions of south-east Europe. Only the male has the yellow forehead, the female's is silver-grey. The feet have only three toes.

White-backed Woodpecker, *Dendrocopus leucotos,* 10 in. Found in Scandinavia, east Europe and further eastwards to east Asia.

Grey-headed Woodpecker, *Picus canus,* 10 in. Breeds in parts of Scandinavia, east Europe and further eastwards to east Asia. Only the male has the bright red forehead.

Green Woodpecker, *Picus viridis,* 12½ in.

(above) Three-toed Woodpecker;
White-backed Woodpecker
(centre) Grey-headed Woodpecker
(below) Green Woodpecker; Black Woodpecker

Ivory-billed Woodpecker; Great Slaty Woodpecker; Greater Yellow-naped Woodpecker

Breeds in the greater part of Europe, except the most northerly regions, as well as in west Asia. It lives mostly in deciduous woods, and feeds mainly on wood ants, but in the autumn it also takes rowan berries.

Black Woodpecker, *Dryocopus martius*, 18 in. Breeds in woods in Norway, Sweden, Finland, and from eastern France eastwards right to Japan and China; also in north Spain. It often drums on a barkless hollow stem. The nest is excavated often very high up in a tree. Only the male has the red nape patch.

Ivory-billed Woodpecker, *Campephilus principalis*, 20 in. Once found in the forests of south-east North America, but now almost extinct apart from a few in Louisiana. It lives mainly on insects and berries.

Great Slaty Woodpecker, *Mulleripicus*

pulverulentus, 20 in. Found in south-east Asia. It feeds largely on ants.

Greater Yellow-naped Woodpecker, *Picus flavinucha,* 13 in. Found in large areas of east Asia.

Pampas Flicker; Red-headed Woodpecker

87

Woodpeckers

(*above*) Yellow-bellied Sapsucker; Cape Gilded Flicker; (*centre*) Little Spotted Woodpecker; (*below*) Ground Woodpecker

Pampas Flicker, *Colaptes campestris,* 12½ in. Found on the pampas of South America, where it eats ants and termites.

Red-headed Woodpecker, *Melanerpes erythrocephalus,* 9½ in. One of the best-known birds in North America, partly owing to its characteristic plumage and partly because it lives on the edges of woods in cultivated areas. It feeds on beetles, grasshoppers and flies, which it often hunts in the air and takes like a flycatcher. In the autumn and winter it feeds on seeds and berries.

Yellow-bellied Sapsucker, *Sphyrapicus varius,* 8½ in. Found in the eastern United States. It hacks hundreds of holes or removes the bark in rings round tree trunks, so that the sap oozes out. This it then licks up with its short tongue which has a brush of fine hairy bristles at the tip. The sap attracts many insects, mostly ants, which are also eaten.

Cape Gilded Flicker, *Colaptes chrysoides,* 13 in. Found in California and Arizona.

Little Spotted Woodpecker, *Campethera cailliauti,* 7 in. Found in the forests of east Africa; it feeds largely on ants and termites.

Ground Woodpecker, *Geocolaptes olivaceus,* 9¾ in. Found in South Africa; it feeds on the ground, mostly on insects.

Wryneck, *Jynx torquilla,* 6½ in. Together with an African species the wryneck makes up the second sub-family of woodpeckers. Breeds in most of Europe, in north-west Africa and in large parts of Asia eastwards to China and Japan. It winters in tropical Africa. The tongue is long and sticky, the neck can be twisted and turned like a snake.

Wryneck

Jacamars

The jacamars, Galbulidae, contain about 15 species, which resemble bee-eaters and kingfishers. They are found rather rarely in damp forest areas from south Mexico to Paraguay and south Brazil. They sit quietly and motionless on a branch and wait for a passing insect, perhaps a butterfly, then they fly out after it and bring it back to the branch to wait for the next prey. They nest in holes which they dig in slopes.

Rufous-tailed Jacamar, *Galbula ruficauda*, 8¾ in. Found in Guiana, Venezuela, Colombia, north Brazil and Trinidad. It feeds on butterflies and other flying insects.

White-billed Jacamar, *Galbula albirostris*, 8¾ in. Found in northern South America.

Swallow Puff-bird; White-breasted Puff-bird

Puff-birds

In spite of their appearance the puff-birds, Bucconidae, are closely related to the jacamars; they have about 32 species varying in size from a sparrow to a shrike, and are found from the southern parts of Mexico to north Argentina. They are unusually sluggish birds, which sit almost motionless, apparently without being aware of their surroundings. In practice they move only when they leave their perch to catch butterflies and other insects; they catch the prey in the same manner as the last group. Most puff-birds breed in tree holes, but some dig nests in slopes.

Swallow Puff-bird, *Chelidoptera tenebrosa*, 6½ in. Lives on the edges of woods in northern South America.

White-breasted Puff-bird, *Malacoptila fusca*, 7½ in. A common forest bird in tropical South America.

(above) Rufous-tailed Jacamar
(below) White-billed Jacamar

89

Swifts

THE SWIFTS, Apodiformes, consist of over 400 small birds, of which the majority are truly dwarf. They feed on insects or nectar which they take when flying or hovering. The wing feathers are much elongated, so that the wings are very long and narrow.

The swifts may be divided into two sub-orders which are very different in outward appearance: the true swifts and the humming birds.

True Swifts

The true swifts, Apodidae, consist of some 80 species. They occur nearly everywhere, except in the polar regions, and most are found in the tropics. The wings are long and narrow and the feet small and weak, so that the birds are almost helpless on the ground. Swifts feed exclusively on flying insects, which they hunt from very early morning to late in the evening. They are believed to spend the night in the air and ean probably sleep while doi ngso. The development of the young lasts for up to six weeks.

Swift, *Apus apus*, 6½ in. Breeds throughout Europe, except in the most northerly regions, and also in north Asia, and winters in south Africa. Said to fly at speeds of over 60 m.p.h.
Chimney Swift, *Chaetura pelagica*, 5 in. Breeds in North America and migrates in autumn in enormous flocks to South America. One of the fastest of all birds and said to fly at speeds up to 85 m.p.h.
Alpine Swift, *Apus melba*, 8¼ in. Breeds at high altitudes in south Europe, Africa and India, usually on steep cliff walls, and often in colonies.
Palm Swift, *Cypsiurus parvus*, 5 in. Widespread in Africa and south Asia.

(above) Swift; Chimney Swift; *(below)* Alpine Swift; Palm Swift

high up on a thin branch and the single egg is stuck to the bottom of the nest.

Whiskered Swift, *Hemiprocne mystacea,* 11½ in. Found in New Guinea, but a similar though much smaller bird occurs in Malaysia.

Humming-birds

The humming-birds, Trochilidae, form a family of about 300 species, many of which are among the most beautiful of all birds, and the smallest; the smallest of all weighs only $\frac{3}{5}$ oz. The wings are long and narrow, the feet small. They can move the wings at a speed of up to 70 beats per second and can hover and manoeuvre like insects. The breast muscles, the breastbone keel and the heart are proportionately larger than in any other bird. Most species are found in South America, but the total distribution of the group is from Arctic North

(above) Glossy Swiftlet; Whiskered Swift
(below) White-rumped Swift

It builds its nest on the outer part of palm leaves and sticks the eggs to the nest with spit.
Glossy Swiftlet, *Collocalia esculenta,* 3½ in. Found in south-east Asia and Indonesia. It builds a nest in caves using plant material, but other swiftlets build nests exclusively of thickened spit and these are the so-called edible birds' nests.
White-rumped Swift, *Apus caffer,* 6 in. Found in tropical Africa.

Tree Swifts

The tree swifts, Hemiprocnidae, consist of three species, all found in the Indo-Australian region. They build a nest

(above) Calliope Humming-bird
(centre) Ruby-throated Humming-bird
(below) Blue-throated Humming-bird

(above) Bourcier's Hermit; Common Sickle-bill; Little Wood-star; Frilled Coquette; Giant Humming-bird; *(below)* Sword-billed Humming-bird; Brazilian Swallow-tail

America (in summer) to southernmost South America. Humming-birds live on insects and nectar. They can catch insects like a flycatcher or find them in flowers. The main food is nectar, which they get by inserting the bill into the flower corolla, whilst they hover and suck with the tubular tongue.

Loddiges' Spatule-tail

Calliope Humming-bird, *Stellula calliope,* 3 in. Breeds from Canada to California and is the commonest humming-bird in the U.S.A.

Ruby-throated Humming-bird, *Archilochus colubris,* 3½ in. Breeds in eastern North America and winters in Mexico and central America.

Blue-throated Humming-bird, *Lampornis clemenciae,* 5 in. Found mainly in Mexico, but occurs in southern U.S.A.

Bourcier's Hermit, *Phaetornis bourcieri,* 5 in. Found in South America.

Common Sickle-bill, *Eutoxeres aquila,* 5 in. Found in Colombia and Ecuador.

Little Wood-star, *Acestrura bombus,* 2¼ in. Found in Ecuador and Peru. The smallest bird in the world.

Frilled Coquette, *Lophornis magnifica,* 4¾ in. Found in Brazil.

Giant Humming-bird, *Patagona gigas,*

6¼ in. Found in Ecuador, Peru, Bolivia and Chile.

Sword-billed Humming-bird, *Ensifera ensifera,* 8½ in. Found in northern South America.

Brazilian Swallow-tail, *Eupetomena macroura,* 7¼ in. Found in the Guianas and Brazil.

Loddiges' Spatule-tail, *Loddigesia mirabilis,* 4¾ in. Known only from the Andes of north Peru from 7-9,000 ft.

White-footed Racket-tail, *Ocreatus underwoodi,* 6 in., from the mountain regions of Venezuela and Colombia, has downy white pantaloons on the feet.

Crimson Topaz, *Topaza pella,* 3½ in., from Guiana and north Brazil, has a topaz-yellow throat.

Sappho Comet, *Sappho sparganura,* 6½ in., from Bolivia and Argentina.

White-headed Mousebird; Red-faced Mousebird

White-footed Racket-tail; Crimson Topaz
(below) Sappho Comet

Colies

THE COLIES or mousebirds, Coliiformes, contain only one family with about 6 species; most are the size of a starling or somewhat smaller. They are sometimes called mousebirds, because the feathers on the body are short, greyish and hair-like, and they also climb about like mice. All the toes can be turned forwards. The wings are short, but in spite of this they fly fast. Colies live in Africa south of the Sahara, principally on bushy steppes with sparse tree growth. They feed mostly on fruits and may do damage in orchards and plantations by eating oranges, tomatoes and avocado pears.

White-headed Mousebird, *Colius leucocephalus,* 13 in. Found in east Africa.

Red-faced Mousebird, *Colius indicus,* 13 in. Found in south-east Africa.

Trogons

THE TROGONS, Trogoniformes, are a small isolated order, containing only one family of 34 species. They differ from other birds in having both the inner toe and the back toe—that is toes number one and two—turning backwards. The males usually have very beautiful plumage, whilst the female's plumage is more modest. Trogons live in tropical rain forests, mostly in America, but also in Asia and Africa. Their skin is remarkably thin, and the feathers are loosely fixed. They are slow, sluggish birds and fly poorly. They are seen either singly or in pairs, but never in flocks. The American species feed on soft fruits, the others on insects. Most breed in tree holes, but some dig holes in earthy banks and others excavate their nest in termite colonies.

(above) Quetzal; Citreoline Trogon; Coppery-tailed Trogon; Narina's Trogon
(centre) Ward's Trogon; Scarlet-rumped Trogon; *(below)* Cuban Trogon

Quetzal, *Pharomachrus mocino,* 50 in. Lives in the mountain forests of central and south America and is the national bird of Guatemala. Two of the male's fringed tail covert feathers may reach a length of more than 3 ft. When the bird sees a fruit, it flies to it, hovers while plucking it and then returns with it to its perch.

Citreoline Trogon, *Trogon citreolus,* 11 in. Found in Mexico and central America.

Coppery-tailed Trogon, *Trogon elegans,* 11½ in. Breeds in Mexico and in some of the southern United States.

Narina's Trogon, *Apaloderma narina,* 11 in. Widely distributed in the forests of east and south Africa.

Ward's Trogon, *Harpactes wardi,* 13½ in. Found in the mountains of northern South-east Asia at heights of 8,000-9,000 ft.

Scarlet-rumped Trogon, *Harpactes duvaucelii,* 9¾ in. Found in southern Asia.

Cuban Trogon, *Priotelus temnurus,* 9¾ in. Very common in the forests of Cuba, where it feeds on berries, flowers and insects.

Coraciae

THE ORDER CORACIIFORMES is a collection of very varied groups, including the hoopoes, hornbills, todies, motmots, bee-eaters, kingfishers, rollers, courols and ground-rollers.

Hoopoes

The hoopoes have long, sometimes curved bills and live in the warmer

Hoopoe

parts of Europe, Asia and Africa. The female nests in tree holes, and the male feeds her during the incubation period.

Hoopoe, *Upupa epops,* 11 in. The large crest running from the inner end of the bill to the nape of the neck can be erected and lowered. Breeds over central and south Europe (rarely in Britain), Africa, Madagascar and the whole of the south part of Asia, and lives mostly in open fields and small woods. It searches through cow dung and carrion for insects and larvae and also takes worms, spiders and other small animals. The hoopoe is shy and wary, and the parents only live together in the breeding season, when they build a nest in a large tree hole, in deserted woodpecker nests or in stone walls. The excretion of the young is not removed from the nest and as the female and the young give off an ill-smelling secretion from the rump gland, there may be a frightful smell in the nest.

Scimitar-bill; White-headed Wood-hoopoe

Asia. The bill is large and thick with a saw-toothed edge and often with a striking horny outgrowth on the upper side. In spite of its size the bill is light, as it is built up of thin bony compartments which are filled with air. In many species the eyelids have long stiff eyelashes. The wings are short and the flight is awkward. Most of them feed on fruits, but many take insects and other animals. They live in pairs mated for life and are sociable birds which often come together in large flocks. Hornbills nest in tree holes, and when the female has laid her eggs, she remains inside and closes up the nest entrance with earth, which the male brings. The cover is almost cement hard, and there is only a vertical slit in it through which she can stick out the tip of her bill. In this way she guards herself and the young against attacks from snakes, apes and other climbing animals. The male feeds the female and later also the young and it is 1-4 months before she chips her way out through the cover and takes over the feeding of the young.

Scimitar-bill, *Rhinopomastus cyanomelas,* 17½ in. Found in tropical east Africa. It feeds mostly on insects, but may also take small fruits. It breeds in tree holes, and both the nest and the birds have a pungent smell like the hoopoe.

White-headed Wood-hoopoe, *Phoenicullus bollei,* 17½ in. Found in central Africa. Like the previous species this is one of the wood-hoopoes.

Hornbills

The hornbills or Bucerotidae consist of over 50 species varying in size from shrike to turkey. They are distributed in Africa south of the Sahara, in south Asia and on the islands of south-east

Indian Pied Hornbill, *Anthracoceros malabaricus,* 30 in. Lives in small noisy flocks in the woods of India and parts of south-east Asia.

White-thighed Hornbill, *Bycanistes albotibialis,* 38 in. Found in the forests of tropical west Africa and feeds on fruits. Like most other hornbills it breeds in high trees.

Silvery-cheeked Hornbill, *Bycanistes brevis,* 35 in. Found in east Africa and feeds exclusively on fruits. The female is almost four months in the nest and comes out together with the fledglings.

Rhinoceros Hornbill, *Buceros rhinoceros,* 42 in. Common in Malaya, Sumatra, Java and Borneo.

HORNBILLS

(above) Indian Pied Hornbill; White-thighed Hornbill; Silvery-cheeked Hornbill
(centre) Rhinoceros Hornbill; Wreathed Hornbill
(below) Abyssinian Ground Hornbill; Great Indian Hornbill

(above) Grey Hornbill
(below) Red-billed Hornbill

Grey Hornbill, *Tockus nasutus,* 15½ in., is the size of a shrike and has no casque on the bill. It is found in Africa and breeds in holes in cliffs, but walls in the nest opening like the other hornbills.

Red-billed Hornbill, *Tockus erythro-rhynchus,* 17 in. Common in central Africa, where it feeds on locusts and other insects. It has no casque.

Todies

The todies, Todidae, are a small group of birds, about the size of blue tits, which are confined to the Greater Antilles. They live on the outskirts of woods and sit on the lookout for insects which they catch and then return to their perch. They dig a nest hole with their bill in slopes.

Broad-billed Tody, *Todus subulatus,* 4½ in. Found in Hispaniola.

Cuban Tody, *Todus multicolor,* 4½ in. Common in the woods of Cuba.

Broad-billed Tody; Cuban Tody

Wreathed Hornbill, *Aceros undulatus,* 39 in. Found in south-east Asia, often in large numbers.

Great Indian Hornbill, *Buceros bicornis,* 45 in. Found in the forests of India and south-east Asia. It feeds on fruits, small mammals and reptiles. When it eats it tosses each piece of food up in the air, catches it with the bill and then swallows it.

Abyssinian Ground Hornbill, *Bucorvus abyssinicus,* 39 in. Found in tropical Africa from Gambia to Uganda. This and a related species are the only hornbills which live mainly on the ground. They have powerful legs and are found in flocks on the savannas where they feed on insects, frogs, snakes, lizards, small mammals and carrion; they also eat fruits. They nest in hollow trees, but the females is not walled in, as with the other hornbills.

Common Motmot; Turquoise-browed Motmot

Motmots

The motmots, Momotidae, are shrike-sized birds with fine tooth-like edges to the bill, short wings and a long tail. The centre pair of tail feathers is the longest and it lacks a piece of the vane a little way back from the tip. It is the birds themselves which bite off these feather barbs. The motmots are quiet birds which live in thick forests in Mexico, central and south America. They often sit and swing the tail back and forwards like a pendulum. The food consists mainly of insects, which they catch in the air. They nest in holes, which they dig deep into slopes.

Common Motmot, *Momotus momota,* 15½ in. Found in the forests of Guiana and north Brazil.

Turquoise-browed Motmot, *Eumomota superciliosa,* 13 in. Found in south Mexico and central America.

Bee-eaters

The bee-eaters, Meropidae, contain about 25 species varying in size from a swallow to a thrush; they have slender pointed wings and long tails, which have 12 feathers. They live in Europe, Asia, Africa and Australia and mainly in tropical regions. The food consists exclusively of insects, by far the greater part being bees and wasps, which they catch in the air and swallow without first removing the sting and without being affected by the poison. Where there is considerable bee-farming they may naturally do some damage. Bee-eaters nest in colonies in cliffs, where they dig long horizontal tunnels with their bill. After the breeding season they fly around in flocks in places where there is plenty of food.

Carmine Bee-eater, *Merops nubicus,* 13 in. Breeds in colonies in tropical Africa, from Senegal to Abyssinia, and feeds on locusts.

Carmine Bee-eater; *(below)* Bee-eater

(above) Blue-bearded Bee-eater
(below) Blue-headed Bee-eater;
Swallow-tailed Bee-eater

Bee-eater, *Merops apiaster,* 11 in. Widespread as a breeding bird in the countries of the Mediterranean and west Asia, sometimes straying northwards to central and north Europe. Unlike most other bee-eaters they are migratory and winter in tropical Africa. The bee-eater is an active bird which can eat double its own weight of insects in a day.

Blue-bearded Bee-eater, *Nyctyornis athertoni,* 13½ in. Found in the forests of India, Burma and Siam.

Blue-headed Bee-eater, *Mellitophagus mulleri,* 7¾ in. Found in the rain forests of Africa.

Swallow-tailed Bee-eater, *Dicrocercus hirundineus,* 8¼ in. Found in Africa from Kenya and Angola southwards.

Kingfishers

The kingfishers, Halcyonidae, consist of over 100 species, of which the majority are found in the tropics, very unequally distributed, mostly in the Indo-Australian region. Most are the size of a sparrow to a thrush, some are about as big as a crow. The body is powerful, the head large, the neck short, the wings proportionately short, and the tail usually very short; the bill is usually long, slender and pointed, and the feet are small and weak. The primitive species are woodland birds, which feed on insects, lizards and small rodents. The more advanced species have developed into diving fish-eaters. The primitive kingfishers wait for their prey from the shelter of trees, from which they fly down to the earth, grab the prey with the bill and fly back to their perch to eat it. The more advanced ones sit on a branch which stretches out over a lake or stream and dive into the water after fish, which they grip with the bill and take back to the branch; here they throw the fish up into the air and catch it in such a way that they can swallow it head first. Some species hover in the air over the water like terns. The fish-eating species breed in holes in the earth 1½-3 ft. long, which they dig in river banks with the bill. The woodland kingfishers breed either in slopes or tree holes, sometimes also in woodpecker holes.

Kingfisher, *Alcedo atthis,* 6½ in. The only species which is found in Europe, where it occurs almost everywhere except in the most northerly regions. To the south it ranges through Africa and India to Indonesia. It dives after small fish, aquatic insects and crustaceans and has its nest in river banks, where it digs out the long horizontal tunnel and nest with its bill. The 6-7 gleaming

(above) Kingfisher; Galatea Racket-tail
(centre) Pied Kingfisher; Laughing Kookaburra; Stork-billed Kingfisher
(below) Green Kingfisher; Belted Kingfisher; White-headed Kingfisher

white eggs are laid without an underlay, but are surrounded by a circle of regurgitated fish bones.

Galatea Racket-tail, *Tanysiptera galatea,* 11 in. Widely distributed in New Guinea. It feeds mostly on millipedes and lizards, which it finds down on the forest floor.

Pied Kingfisher, *Ceryle rudis,* 10¼ in. Widespread in Africa south of the Sahara, in west Asia and particularly common along the whole of the Nile.

Laughing Kookaburra, *Dacelo novaeguineae,* 18 in. Found in Australia and

New Guinea and well known for its high laughing voice. It feeds on rodents, lizards, snakes, crabs and insects.

Stork-billed Kingfisher, *Pelargopsis capensis,* 14½ in. Widely distributed in India and Burma along rivers and small streams. It feeds on fish, lizards, frogs, crabs, insects, and even young birds.

Green Kingfisher, *Chloroceryle americana,* 7 in. Extends from the southern United States into many parts of South America.

Belted Kingfisher, *Megaceryle alcyon,* 12½ in. Breeds in Alaska and north

(*above*) Crab-eating Kingfisher;
Malay Forest Kingfisher
(*below*) Pigmy Kingfisher;
Grey-headed Kingfisher

Canada and winters in the West Indies
and United States.

White-headed Kingfisher, *Halcyon sau-
rophaga,* 13½ in. Lives in New Guinea and
neighbouring islands.

Crab-eating Kingfisher, *Clytoceyx rex,*
12½ in. Found in New Guinea, where it
feeds on crabs in mangrove swamps.

Malay Forest Kingfisher, *Ceyx rufi-
dorsum,* 7¾ in. Found in the forests of
Malaya and Indonesia.

Pigmy Kingfisher, *Ispidina picta,* 5 in.
Found along the roads in tropical
Africa south of the Sahara.

Grey-headed Kingfisher, *Halcyon leucocephala pallidiventris,* 8¾ in. Found along
the rivers in East Africa, Angola and
Rhodesia.

Rollers

The rollers, ground-rollers and courols
have a thick body, a large head and a
powerful bill.

The rollers, Coraciidae, somewhat
resemble the crows in form and size but
are more brightly coloured. Most are
found in Africa, but there are also
species in the Indo-Malaysian and
Australian regions, as well as a single
one in Europe. They live up in the
tree-tops, where they sit on a branch on
the lookout for prey—usually lizards,
frogs, small rodents, grasshoppers,
beetles and other insects which they
catch and then take back to the branch.
They lay their eggs in tree holes, cliff
crevices, earth holes, termite colonies
or in deserted starling and woodpecker
holes, and often breed in colonies. The
male and the female take it in turns to
incubate the eggs and tend the young.

Indian Roller, *Coracias benghalensis,* 12½

(*above*) Indian Roller
(*below*) Roller

in. Widely distributed in open country in South Asia.

Roller, *Coracias garrulus*, 12 in. Breeds in east-central and south Europe and in west Asia, and winters in Africa and north-west India. It lives mostly in light and open woodland, where it nests in tree holes. It feeds mainly on beetles, grasshoppers and other larger insects, but may also take larvae, worms, frogs and lizards.

Broad-billed Roller, *Eurystomus orientalis,* 11¾ in. Widely distributed in the Indian and Australian regions. It spends long periods of the day motionless on a branch, most often in a free-standing tree, but in the morning and evening it hunts actively for insects, often together with bats. It lays its eggs high up in hollow trees.

Lilac-breasted Roller, *Coracias caudatc*, 15 in. Found in east and parts of south Africa. It feeds both on small birds and snakes.

(above) Courol
(below) Short-legged Ground-roller

Courols

Courol, *Leptosomus discolor*, 17 in. Found in Madagascar and the Comoros, where it lives in trees on the edges of forests; this is the only species in the family Leptosomatidae. It feeds on larvae and insects, but may also take small lizards.

Ground-rollers

The ground-rollers, Brachypteraciidae, with five species, are found in Madagascar and the Comoros.

Short-legged Ground-roller, *Brachypteracias leptosomus*, 13 in. Lives on the forest floor in thick rain forests and feeds on insects, chameleons and small snakes.

(above) Broad-billed Roller
(below) Lilac-breasted Roller

Nightjars

THE NIGHTJARS and their relatives, Caprimulgiformes, are a group of some 100 species with broad mouths and short flat beaks with stiff bristles at the base. The plumage is soft, the wings long and the feet small. Most are nocturnal, and feed exclusively on insects which they catch in the air. As a rule they have a purring voice. The order contains the true nightjars, frogmouths, goatsuckers, owlet nightjars and oil-birds.

True Nightjars

True nightjars, Caprimulgidae, are found nearly everywhere in the warmer regions, mostly in central and south America. They are slender birds, the feet are weak and the birds often lie prone on horizontal branches. The food consists exclusively of flying insects, amongst others moths and cockchafers. Nightjars nest on the ground without making any hollow, still less a nest, and lay 1-2 eggs. Certain species hibernate in cliff crevices, and at this time their body temperature may drop to about 66° F.

Nightjar, *Caprimulgus europaeus*, 12½ in. Breeds throughout almost the whole of Europe, in north-west Africa and west Asia, and many winter in east and south Africa. They start to hunt insects at twilight; about half the food consists of moths, and is otherwise mainly beetles. The Latin name, *Caprimulgus*, means goat-milker; in the old days it was thought that the bird flew around at night-time and milked goats and cows, because it was so often seen fluttering around farm animals in the evening when hunting for insects.
Egyptian Nightjar, *Caprimulgus aegyptius*, 10¼ in. Found in south-western Asia and extending to parts of north Africa.
Whip-poor-will, *Caprimulgus vociferus*, 9½ in. Named after its characteristic call. It breeds from south Canada to the southern United States.

(above) Nightjar; Egyptian Nightjar; *(centre)* Whip-poor-will
(below) Common Nighthawk; Dusky Nightjar

(*above*) Brazilian Nighthawk
(*below*) Standard-wing Nightjar; Pennant-wing Nightjar

Common Nighthawk, *Chordeiles minor*, 11 in. Breeds in south Canada and the United States. It dives down from great heights and feeds on insects.
Dusky Nightjar, *Caprimulgus pectoralis*, 9 in. Found from Uganda and Kenya to South Africa.
Brazilian Nighthawk, *Macropsalis creagra*, 31 in. Found in the forests of southeast Brazil.
Standard-wing Nightjar, *Macrodipteryx longipennis*, 8¾ in. Found in many parts of tropical Africa. One of the wing feathers is 15 in. long, with a vane only in the outermost part. When in flight the bird looks as though it is being followed by two small bats.
Pennant-wing Nightjar, *Semeiophorus vexillarius*, 11 in. Found from Angola and Tanganyika to south Africa, and more diurnal than the other nightjars. One pair of wing feathers is greatly elongated, over 18 in.
White-necked Nighthawk, *Nyctidromus albicollis*, 9¾-11¾ in. Widely distributed in the tropical forests of south America but seldom observed.

Frogmouths

The frogmouths, Podargidae, have short bills and incredibly broad gapes. They are found in the forests of Australia and east Asia and feed on insects on the ground.

Tawny Frogmouth; (*below*) Large Frogmouth

(left, from above) White-necked Nighthawk; Giant Goatsucker
(right) Owlet Nightjar; Bennett's Owlet Nightjar

Tawny Frogmouth, *Podargus strigoides,* 19½ in. Found in Australia and Tasmania. It hunts insects at night and may also take tree-frogs and young birds.

Large Frogmouth, *Batrachostomus auritus,* 15¾ in. Found in Malaya, Sumatra and Borneo.

Goatsuckers

The goatsuckers, Nyctibiidae, are all found in the tropical forests of central and south America. They hunt insects in the air at night-time.

Giant Goatsucker, *Nyctibius griseus,* 13½ in. Widely distributed but seldom seen.

Owlet Nightjars

The owlet nightjars, Aegothelidae, are found principally in New Guinea and Australia. They resemble small owls in appearance and habits.

Owlet Nightjar, *Aegotheles cristatus,* 8½ in. Found in Australia.

Bennett's Owlet Nightjar, *Aegotheles bennetti,* 9½ in. Found in New Guinea.

Oil-birds

Oil-bird, *Steatornis caripensis,* 21½ in. The only species in the family Steatornithidae, it is found in large colonies in caves in South America. It eats fruits and can fly in complete darkness. The nestlings are incredibly fat.

Oil-bird

(from left) Barn Owl; Masked Owl; Cape Grass-owl; Sooty Owl

Owls

THE OWLS, Strigiformes, with some 150 species, are represented in all parts of the world except Antarctica and vary in size from a sparrow to a buzzard. The eyes face forwards and their sight, which is adapted for twilight, is very good. The ear opening is large, and their hearing is better than that of any other birds. When it starts to get dark owls begin to hunt for insects or other small invertebrates. They nest in tree holes or large deserted birds' nests. The eggs are round and white, and incubation starts when the first egg has been laid. The order contains two families: the barn owls and the true owls.

Barn Owls

The barn owls have a heart-shaped feather ring round the eyes.

Barn Owl, *Tyto alba,* 13½ in. Widespread over nearly the whole of the earth. Unlike other owls it catches many shrews. It breeds in churches and barns, almost without an underlay.

Masked Owl, *Tyto castanops,* 17 in. Found in Australia and Tasmania, usually in open woods.

(above) Tengmalm's Owl
(centre) Hawk Owl; Little Owl
(below) Pigmy Owl

107

(from left) Long-eared Owl; Short-eared Owl; <u>Scops Owl</u>; Tawny Owl

Cape Grass-owl, *Tyto capensis,* 13½ in. Found in southern Africa. It has its nest on the ground in high grass.
Sooty Owl, *Tyto tenebricosa,* 13¼ in. Found in the forests of New Guinea and parts of Australia.

(above) Burrowing Owl; Elf Owl
(below) Boobook Owl; Spectacled Owl

True Owls

The feather ring round the eyes is circular, and the eyes are proportionately large.

Tengmalm's Owl, *Aegolius funereus,* 10 in. Found in the conifer areas of Scandinavia and east Europe, where it feeds principally on small rodents. It often breeds in old woodpecker nests or in hollow trees.
Hawk Owl, *Surnia ulula,* 15 in. Found in the conifer forests of Scandinavia and north Russia, where it feeds on lemmings and other small rodents; by day it hunts small birds.
Little Owl, *Athene noctua,* 8½ in. Breeds in Asia, north Africa and Europe, except in the more northerly regions. It feeds on mice, small birds, insects and earthworms and breeds in church towers and hollow trees.
Pygmy Owl, *Glaucidium passerinum,* 6½ in. Breeds in north and east Europe and into east Asia. It feeds on mice and large insects and breeds in tree holes.

Long-eared Owl, *Asio otus*, 14 in. Widespread in the temperate belt of the northern hemisphere and very common in conifer woods. It feeds mostly on mice but also on small birds and usually breeds in old crow or buzzard nests.

Short-eared Owl, *Asio flammeus*, 15 in. Widely distributed over almost the whole of the northern hemisphere as well as in central and south America. It hunts both in twilight and in daylight and feeds mostly on field mice.

Scops Owl, *Otus scops*, 7½ in. Found in Mediterranean countries and in Asia.

Tawny Owl, *Strix aluco*, 15 in. Widespread in deciduous forest areas in Europe and Asia. When it becomes dark, they fly out to hunt for mice and may now and then get their claws into small birds. They breed in hollow trees or holes in buildings.

Burrowing Owl, *Speotyto cunicularia*, 9 in. Found in the western United States, where it nests in colonies in holes dug in the ground by prairie dogs; also common in South America. They often sit outside the nest hole; by night they catch mice, frogs and insects.

Elf Owl, *Micrathene whitneyi*, 6 in. The smallest of all the owls; it is found in western U.S.A., and feeds on insects. It nests in holes in large cactus plants.

Boobook Owl, *Ninox theomacha*, 10¼ in. Found in the mountain forests of New Guinea up to heights of 3,500 ft.

Spectacled Owl, *Pulsatrix perspicillata*, 17½-19½ in. Found in forests from Mexico to South America.

Great Horned Owl, *Bubo virginianus*, 23-32 in. Widespread in both north and south America. Feeds amongst other things on cats, skunks and fowl.

Eagle Owl, *Bubo bubo*, 27 in. Lives in the mountain forest regions in the greater part of Europe, and feeds on small rodents but also takes hares, partridges, crows and ducks, usually at twilight.

(above, from left) Eagle Owl; Great Horned Owl
(centre) Brown Fish Owl
(below, from left) Ural Owl; Lapland Owl

Parrots

(from left) Snowy Owl; Fishing Owl

Brown Fish Owl, *Bubo zeylonensis,* 21 in. Found in forest country in India, Ceylon, south-east India and south-east China. It eats mostly frogs, fish and crustaceans.
Ural Owl, *Strix uralensis,* 24 in. Breeds in the conifer forest regions of east Europe and Asia. It can hunt by daylight and lives mostly on lemmings and other small rodents.
Lapland Owl, *Strix nebulosa,* 27 in. Breeds in the conifer forest regions of the northern hemisphere, and feeds largely on lemmings.
Snowy Owl, *Nyctea scandiaca,* 21-26 in. Breeds in the Arctic, but may move southwards in winter, sometimes in large numbers. The female is larger and more powerful than the male. Snowy owls most often hunt by day and feed on lemmings and other small rodents, as well as hares and ptarmigan. They breed on small humps in tundra or heath.
Fishing Owl, *Scotopelia peli,* 25 in. Found throughout tropical Africa.

THE PARROTS, Psittaciformes, are a well-defined order of tropical birds, with a single family containing over 300 species. The root of the bill with the nostrils is covered by naked skin. The beak can be used as a nutcracker and also as a rasp, because the lower bill can be moved back and forwards against the underside of the upper bill, which is provided with transverse horny ridges. Parrots climb well and use the hook of the beak as a kind of third foot. Two of the toes turn forwards and two backwards. The brain is relatively large and parrots are probably more intelligent than other birds. They talk well, but naturally do not understand what they are saying—they are exclusively mimics.

Parrots are found in Africa, Asia, Australia, north and south America, being most numerous in the Australian region and south America. The majority live in trees and feed on fruits and seeds, but some take roots, honey, insects or larvae. They mate for life and are very affectionate. Some parrots may live for 50-80 years.

Macaws

The macaws are the largest of the parrots and are found in the forests of central and south America from Mexico to south Brazil. They have a strong curved bill, powerful enough to crack a brazil-nut.

Scarlet Macaw, *Ara macao,* 36 in. Found from Mexico to south Brazil.
Blue Macaw, *Anodorhynchus hyacinthinus,* 38 in. Found in Brazil south of the Amazon, this is the world's largest parrot. The food consists of palm kernels, nuts and fruits. It breeds in holes in the river banks.

(above) Scarlet Macaw; Blue Macaw; Blue-and-yellow Macaw; Military Macaw
(then, on left from above) Hawk-headed Caique; Greater Vasa Parrot; Grey Parrot
(on right, from above) Smaller Patagonian Conure; Cuban Parrot; Blue-fronted Parrot;
Yellow-headed Conure

(above) Budgerigar; Crimson Parrakeet; Red Lory; Tahiti Blue Lory
(below) Green Ground Parrot

Blue-and-yellow Macaw, *Ara ara-rauna,* 36 in. Found mainly in northern South America.
Military Macaw, *Ara militaris,* 27 in. Found from Mexico to Bolivia.
Hawk-headed Caique, *Deroptyus accipitrinus,* 13½ in. Found in the forests of Amazonia.

(above) Long-tailed Parrakeet
(below) New Guinea Eclectus Parrot,
female and male

Greater Vasa Parrot, *Coracopsis vasa,* 19½ in. Found in Madagascar and the Comoros.
Grey Parrot, *Psittacus erithacus,* 12 in. Very common in west Africa and east to Tanganyika. It breeds in tree holes in mangrove forests and does damage by eating half-ripe maize. This is a common parrot in captivity and talks well.
Smaller Patagonian Conure, *Cyanoliseus patagonus,* 17½ in. Found in southeastern South America.
Cuban Parrot, *Amazona leucocephala,* 12¼ in. Found in the West Indies.
Blue-fronted Parrot, *Amazona aestiva,* 13½ in. Found in the rain forests of South America south of the Amazon, and common as a cage bird.
Yellow-headed Conure, *Aratinga jandaya,* 11½ in. Lives in flocks in the forests of east Brazil and does much damage in rice and maize plantations.
Budgerigar, *Melopsittacus undulatus,* 7½ in. Found in large flocks in open country in Australia, where it feeds on seeds. The male has a blue waxy skin, the female brown. The budgerigar is by far the commonest cage bird among the

(above) Great Black Cockatoo; Rose-crested Cockatoo; Banksian Cockatoo
(centre) Leadbeater's Cockatoo; Greater Sulphur-crested Cockatoo
(below) Gang Gang Cockatoo; Slender-billed Cockatoo; Cockatiel

parrots and is found in a number of colour variations.

Crimson Parrakeet, *Platycercus elegans,* 14½ in. Found in Australia, where it damages maize plantations.

Red Lory, *Domicella rubra,* 13 in. Found in the Moluccas.

Tahiti Blue Lory, *Vini peruvianus,* 7 in. Found in the Marquesas.

Green Ground Parrot, *Pezoporus wallicus,* 12½ in. Found in Australia.

Long-tailed Parrakeet, *Psittacula krameri,* 15½ in. Found in large flocks in central Africa and India.

New Guinea Eclectus Parrot, *Lorius roratus,* 15½ in. Found in New Guinea and the Moluccas. The male is green, the female red.

Cockatoos

The cockatoos are a well-defined group of parrots found in the Philippines, Moluccas, New Guinea and Australia. They have a large crest on the head which can be raised and lowered. They are often found in forests in flocks.

(above) Kea; Vulturine Parrot
(below) Owl-parrot

Kea, *Nestor notabilis,* 19½ in. Found on South Island, New Zealand at heights of 4,000-6,000 ft. It feeds on plant food and larvae, but may also attack sheep.
Vulturine Parrot, *Psittrichas fulgidus,* 19 in. Found in the mountain forests of New Guinea.
Owl-parrot, *Strigops habroptilus,* 23 in. Found in New Zealand, but now rare. A nocturnal, almost flightless bird.
Rosy-faced Lovebird, *Agapornis roseicollis,* 6¼ in. Found from Angola to the Orange river.
Blue-crowned Hanging Parrakeet, *Loriculus galgulus,* 5 in. Found in Malaya and Indonesia; it sleeps upside down.
Slender-billed Parrot, *Enicognathus leptorhynchus,* 15 in. Found in the forests of Chile, where it digs up corn and roots.
Pigmy Parrot, *Micropsitta keiensis,* 3¾ in. Found in New Guinea. Not much larger than a wren.

Great Black Cockatoo, *Probosciger aterrimus,* 31 in. The largest of the cockatoos. Found on the Aru Islands, in New Guinea and north-east Australia. It has naked cheeks which can change colour.
Rose-crested Cockatoo, *Kakatoe moluccensis,* 19 in., from the southern Moluccas.
Banksian Cockatoo, *Calyptorhynchus magnificus,* 27 in. Found in Australia, but very rare. It feeds on roots and larvae.
Leadbeater's Cockatoo, *Kakatoe leadbeateri,* 15½ in. Found in open woodland in Australia.
Greater Sulphur-crested Cockatoo, *Kakatoe galerita,* 19½ in. Common in Australia from the coasts up to 5,000 ft.
Gang Gang Cockatoo, *Callocephalon fimbriatum,* 13½ in. Lives in the tops of trees in south-east Australia.
Slender-billed Cockatoo, *Kakatoe tenuirostris,* 15½ in. Found in Australia mainly in the west. It uses its bill to dig up roots.
Cockatiel, *Nymphicus hollandicus,* 13 in. Common on the plains of Australia.

(above) Rosy-faced Lovebird; Blue-crowned Hanging Parrakeet; *(centre)* Slender-billed Parrot; *(below)* Pigmy Parrot

(*above*) Emerald Cuckoo; Jamaican Lizard Cuckoo; Cuckoo
(*below*) Yellow-billed Cuckoo; Great Spotted Cuckoo

Cuckoos

THE CUCKOOS, Cuculiformes, consist of some 150 species divided into two families: the true cuckoos and touracos, which are sometimes put into a separate order.

True Cuckoos

The characteristic of the family is the climbing foot with two toes forwards and two backwards. The 130 species are found mainly in the tropics. It should be stressed that the majority build their own nests and look after their own offspring. The family may be divided into tree cuckoos, fruit cuckoos, anis, ground cuckoos and coucals.

All the *tree cuckoos* are parasites, which lay their eggs in the nests of other birds. An individual female always lays her eggs in the nest of a definite bird species. Cuckoo eggs are variously coloured, but one bird always lays eggs of the same pattern. When the naked and blind young hatches out, it pushes itself round in the nest, until it has got an egg or a youngster on its back. Then it works itself backwards up the nest side and casts its load out, and goes on doing this until it alone remains in the nest. The foster parents do not help their own offspring but feed the young cuckoo which may become larger than themselves. The food consists principally of insects; some species also eat frogs, lizards, snakes and young birds.

Cuckoo, *Cuculus canorus,* 13 in. Widely distributed over the whole of Europe and in the temperate and subtropical parts of Asia and Africa. It lives in woods and on commons and is shy and restless. Those that breed in the north spend the winter in tropical Africa; they feed on insects and larvae, mostly hairy caterpillers, and most often lay their eggs in the nests of reed warblers, meadow pipits and wagtails.

Great Spotted Cuckoo, *Clamator glandarius*, 15½ in. Breeds in Africa and south Europe. The eggs are usually laid in a nest of one of the crow family.

Emerald Cuckoo, *Chrysococcyx cupreus*, 9 in. Found in tropical Africa south of the Sahara; it lives high up in the trees.

Koel, *Eudynamys scolopacea*, 17 in. Found in India, with many races in south-east Asia. It feeds on insects and fruits.

Channel-bill, *Scythrops novae-hollandiae*, 25 in. Found from the Lesser Sunda Islands to north-east Australia. It catches insects in the trees, but feeds mostly on fruits, particularly figs.

The *fruit cuckoos* are found in thick rain forests, where they feed on insects and fruits. They build nests and look after their own young.

Yellow-billed Cuckoo, *Coccyzus americanus*, 11 in. Breeds in North America and winters in South America.

Jamaican Lizard Cuckoo, *Saurothera vetula*, 15 in. Found in Jamaica, where it feeds mostly on insects, lizards and mice.

Greater Green-billed Malcoha, *Phoenicophaeus tristis*, 23 in. Found in south Asia, where it feeds on fruit, insects and snails.

The *anis* are found in central and south America. They often run around on the ground or perch on cattle to find insects and larvae. They build communal nests where the females lay their eggs and take it in turn to incubate.

Smooth-billed Ani, *Cratophaga ani*, 14 in. Found in northern South America and the West Indies.

(above) Channel-bill; Guira Cuckoo; Smooth-billed Ani; *(below)* Roadrunner

(above) Greater Green-billed Malcoha; Koel; *(below)* Pheasant Coucal; Greater Coucal

Guira Cuckoo, *Guira guira*, 16 in. Found in South America.

The *ground cuckoos* are fast-running long-legged birds found in open dry country from southern North America to northern South America.

Roadrunner, *Geococcyx californianus*, 23 in. Found in south California and neighbouring states and in Mexico. It feeds on insects, snails and reptiles. In Mexico it is kept half-tame on the farms to catch rattlesnakes.

The *coucals* are long-legged birds which live in scrub and savannas in Africa and Asia. They fly badly but run well, and feed on insects, lizards and snakes.

Pheasant Coucal, *Centropus phasianinus*, 12½ in. Found in Australia and New Guinea.

Greater Coucal, *Centropus sinensis*, 19½ in. Widespread in south Asia.

Touracos

The touracos or plantain-eaters are a group of African birds found principally in the forests south of the Sahara. They vary in size from a dove to a pheasant and feed mostly on flies and fruits, but not particularly on plantains. Touracos keep together in small flocks in the tree-tops.

Blue Touraco, *Corythaeola cristata*, 29 in. Found widespread in the forest regions of west Africa. It builds a nest of twigs on a tree branch and lays 1-2 eggs.

Guinea Touraco, *Turaco persa*, 17½ in. Found in the woods of west Africa.

Hartlaub's Touraco, *Turaco hartlaubi*, 17½ in. Found in the mountain forests of east Africa. So far as possible it avoids strong sunshine, and also heavy rain showers, which may soak the feathers so that it cannot fly.

z

Eastern Grey Plantain-eater, *Crinifer zonurus*, 19 in. Found on the savannas of east Africa. It feeds on fruits, seeds and flowers and rivals the monkeys in noise and activity.

Ross's Touraco, *Musophaga rossae*, 18 in. Found in the rain forests of central Africa; it feeds mostly on figs.

Birds of Prey

THE BIRDS OF PREY, Falconiformes, consist of about 300 species. By far the majority are specialized for living on prey, mainly vertebrates. The bill is short, and the hooked upper mandible of the bill is curved and pointed and has naked waxy skin at its root. They have powerful gripping feet, and the claws are large, hooked and pointed, except in the vultures.

The birds of prey are found widespread over most of the earth and are lacking only in Antarctica and in some islands in the Pacific. The larger species are carrion-eaters or take larger vertebrates, and the majority are very specialized in their type of food. The female is usually larger than the male, and they live in pairs. The young are down-clad, and the male helps with the rearing by collecting food.

The birds of prey may be divided into two sub-orders: the American vultures, which contain only one family, and the true birds of prey, which contain the secretary birds, the falcons, hawks, ospreys and eagles.

(from above) Blue Touraco; Guinea Touraco; Hartlaub's Touraco; Eastern Grey Plantain-eater; Ross's Touraco

American Vultures

The American vultures are found only in North and South America, where they

are widely distributed. The head and neck are naked and the wings relatively large; the sense of smell is very good, and the sense of sight phenomenal. They live largely on carrion.

American King Vulture, *Sarcorhamphus papa*, 34 in. Found in forest-clad hills from south Mexico to north Argentina.
California Condor, *Gymnogyps californianus*, 39 in. Found only in the coastal mountains of California, and now extremely rare.
Great Condor, *Vultur gryphus*, 39 in., with a wing span up to 115 in. It is found in the Andes at heights of 6,000-18,000 ft. and spends most of the day hovering on the lookout for carrion. Exceptionally it takes living llama foals and deer kids.
Black Vulture, *Coragyps atratus*, 23 in. Widespread from southern United States to South America. It feeds largely on carrion, and often frequents heron and pelican colonies, where it eats dead fish and deserted nestlings.

(above, from left) American King Vulture; California Condor; Great Condor
(centre) Black Vulture
(below) Turkey Vulture

Turkey Vulture, *Cathartes aura,* 31 in. Found from south Canada to southern South America.

Secretary Birds

Secretary Bird, *Sagittarius serpentarius,* 49 in. Found on the African savannas south of the Sahara. It has very long legs and the feet are adapted for running and the claws are only slightly curved. The wings are long, and the central tail feathers are 18 in. long. At the back of the neck there are six long feathers which can be erected; they are reminiscent of old-time quill pens which clerks stuck behind their ears. Secretary birds eat small vertebrates and large insects, their main food being snakes which they grip with the beak and trample with the feet. They normally walk or run, but seldom fly.

Secretary Bird

Falcons

The falcons, with some 60 species, mostly have a characteristic sharp "tooth" on the upper mandible, which helps with the division of the prey. The wings are long and pointed, and the wing-beats rapid. They build no nests, but use the deserted nests of other birds or breed on the ground, on cliff ledges or in church towers. In many places they are used for hunting birds, and in the Middle Ages falconry was a favourite sport in Europe.

Prairie Falcon, *Falco mexicanus,* 13½ in. Found on the prairies from southern Canada to south Mexico.
Kestrel, *Falco tinnunculus,* 13½ in. Found in the whole of Europe and Asia, except in the Arctic, as well as parts of Africa. It feeds on mice and insects, and breeds in towers or in the deserted nests of other birds.
Lesser Kestrel, *Falco naumanni,* 12 in. Breeds in the countries of the Mediterranean and further eastward in Asia. It feeds almost exclusively on insects.
Gyr Falcon, *Falco rusticolus,* 20-22 in. Found in the mountain regions of Norway, Sweden, and Russia, as well as in Iceland, Greenland and northern North America. It can catch ptarmigan, gulls and other birds in the air, and takes small rodents on the ground.
Merlin, *Falco columbarius,* 10½-13 in. Found in north Europe and Britain. It feeds on small birds, which it catches in the air.
Caracara, *Polyborus cheriway,* 24 in. Found in southern United States to northern South America. It is often seen on the ground and feeds mostly on carrion.
Hobby, *Falco subbuteo,* 12-14 in. Breeds in most of Europe, Asia and north-west

(above) Prairie Falcon; <u>Kestrel</u>; Lesser Kestrel
(below) Gyr Falcon; Merlin; Caracara

Africa. It is the best flyer amongst the falcons, and can even hunt swallows and martins.

<u>**Peregrine,** *Falco peregrinus,*</u> 15-19 in. Found almost everywhere except in the Antarctic. It flies fast and takes pigeons, partridges, ducks, gulls, sparrow hawks and kestrels. It breeds in old crows, nests or on cliff ledges.

Lanner Falcon, *Falco biarmicus,* 17 in. Found in south Italy, Yugoslavia, Greece, and a large part of Africa.

Saker Falcon, *Falco cherrug,* 18 in. Found on the steppes in south-east Europe and central Asia.

Eleonora's Falcon, *Falco eleonorae,* 15 in, Breeds on islands and cliffs round the Mediterranean.

(from left) Hobby; <u>Peregrine</u>; Lanner Falcon;
Saker Falcon; Eleonora's Falcon; Red-footed Falcon

Osprey

Osprey

Osprey, *Pandion haliaetus,* 20-23 in. The only species in the family Pandionidae. The claws are relatively powerfully hooked, and the outer toe is a turning toe. Ospreys are found in north-east Europe and in many other temperate and tropical regions of the world. They are commonest along sea coasts and feed almost exclusively on fish, which they dive for with outspread claws and folded wings. The nest is built high up in trees.

Hawks and Eagles

A large group containing the Old World vultures as well as the hawks and eagles. They seize and carry the prey with the sharp claws and pull it apart with the hooked bill.

Red-footed Falcon, *Falco vespertinus,* 12 in. Breeds in south Europe, and feeds on insects and small rodents.

(above) Pallid Harrier; Swallow-tailed Kite; Marsh Harrier
(below) Hen Harrier; Montagu's Harrier

(from above) Black-winged Kite;
Everglade Kite; African Marsh Harrier

13 in. Breeds in Africa and south Asia,
and in south Europe.

Everglade Kite, *Rostrhamus sociabilis,*
13½ in. Found from Florida to Argentina; it feeds on snails, frogs and fish.

African Marsh Harrier, *Circus ranivorus,*
18 in. Found in southern Africa.

Black Kite, *Milvus migrans,* 22 in. Found
in central and south Europe, Africa,
south Asia and Australia.

Kite, *Milvus milvus,* 24 in. Found from
south Scandinavia to the Mediterranean,
in north-west Africa and west Asia. It
builds a nest in trees and takes its food
on the ground, mostly mice, reptiles,
insects, carrion and offal.

Honey Buzzard, *Pernis apivorus,* 20-23
in. Found in most of Europe and Africa.
It feeds on wasps, bees and maggots and
also takes frogs and lizards.

Pallid Harrier, *Circus macrourus,* 17-19 in.
Found in east Europe and the temperate
parts of Asia.

Swallow-tailed Kite, *Elanoides forficatus,*
21½ in. Breeds in the southern United
States, where it is often seen in large
flocks. It catches insects in the air.

Marsh Harrier, *Circus aeruginosus,* 19-22
in. Found in Europe and west Asia,
except in the northernmost regions.

Hen Harrier, *Circus cyaneus,* 17-20 in.
Found over most of Europe and Asia.
The female is significantly larger than
the male. Feeds on mice, rats, frogs and
small birds; nests on moors, heathland,
or in swamps.

Montagu's Harrier, *Circus pygargus,*
16-18 in. Found in central and south
Europe, north-west Africa and west
Asia.

Black-winged Kite, *Elanus caeruleus,*

(above) Black Kite
(below) Kite; Honey Buzzard

(above) Fish Eagle; White-bellied Sea Eagle
(below) White-tailed Eagle; Korean Sea Eagle; White-headed Sea Eagle

Sea eagles are widespread almost everywhere except in South America. They are large birds of prey with large broad wings, powerful legs and very strong bills. They feed mainly on fish.

Fish Eagle, *Haliaeetus vocifer*, 27 in. Found from Senegal and Abyssinia to South Africa, usually near rivers and lakes.

White-bellied Sea Eagle, *Haliaeetus leucogaster*, 27 in. Found from India through Indonesia to Australia.

White-tailed Eagle, *Haliaeetus albicilla*, 27-36 in. This, the largest of eagles, is widespread over east Europe and north Asia and is also found in Iceland and Greenland. In addition to fish it takes diving ducks and coots, and exceptionally hares and lambs. It usually builds a nest high up in trees or on cliff ledges.

Korean Sea Eagle, *Haliaeetus pelagicus*, 46 in. Found on Kamtchatka and Sakhalin; it feeds mostly on fish and small mammals.

White-headed Sea Eagle, *Haliaeetus leucocephalus*, 39 in. Found in North America, where, as the national bird of the U.S.A., it is known as the bald eagle.

There are about 40 species of *buzzard* distributed over most of the earth, except Australia. They have broad wings, short tails and relatively slow flight. They catch their prey on the ground and feed on mice and reptiles, sometimes on insects and young birds.

Rough-legged Buzzard, *Buteo lagopus*, 20-24 in. Breeds in mountain regions in the northernmost parts of Europe and Asia, and migrates southwards, mostly to east Europe.

Long-legged Buzzard, *Buteo rufinus*, 24-26 in. A steppe bird, which breeds in the east Mediterranean and further east into Asia.

Buzzard, *Buteo buteo,* 20-22 in. Found nearly everywhere in Europe, and often seen circling in the air with outstretched wings. It builds in high trees or takes over the old nests of other birds.

Black Hawk, *Buteogallus anthracina,* 21 in. Found in southern United States south to northern South America.

Chilean Eagle, *Geranoaetus melanoleucus,* 27 in. A large buzzard found in the greater part of South America.

The *hawks* are small to medium-sized birds with very short wings and long tails. They feed mostly on birds and mammals and also take other prey on the ground.

(*above*) Black Hawk; Goshawk
(*below*) Chilean Eagle

(*above*) Rough-legged Buzzard;
Long-legged Buzzard
(*below*) Buzzard

Goshawk, *Accipiter gentilis,* 19-24 in. Breeds in Europe, except in Britain and Portugal, as well as in Asia and north America. It usually builds a nest in a cleft branch and feeds mostly on wood pigeons, crows, shrikes and fowl. The male is significantly smaller than the female.

Sparrow Hawk, *Accipiter nisus,* 11-15 in. Found nearly everywhere in Europe, north-west Africa and large parts of Asia. It can catch sparrows and other small birds in the air. The male is not much larger than a blackbird; the female is about the size of a pigeon.

Great Sparrow Hawk, *Accipiter melanoleucus,* 18-21 in. Found in the African forests south of the Sahara.

Bateleur Eagle, *Terathopius ecaudatus,* 21 in. Found in Africa south of the Sahara. It feeds on lizards, grasshoppers and carrion.

(above) Sparrow Hawk; Great Sparrow Hawk
(below) Bateleur Eagle

Long-crested Hawk-eagle, *Lophaetus occipitalis,* 21½ in. Found in the forest regions in Africa south of the Sahara.

Bonelli's Eagle, *Hieraetus fasciatus,* 26-29 in. Breeds in south Europe, west Africa and parts of Asia. It feeds on rabbits and birds.

Rufous-bellied Eagle, *Hieraetus kieneri,* 19½ in. Widespread in south Asia, but rare.

The *true eagles* are large brownish birds of prey with feathered legs.

Golden Eagle, *Aquila chrysaëtos,* 30-35 in. Found in mountains and woods in Scotland, north Scandinavia, south Europe, north Asia and north America. It lives in open country, often along the shore, and feeds on hares, squirrels, lambs, deer kids, ducks, geese, fowl and carrion.

Tawny Eagle, *Aquila rapax,* 26-31 in. Breeds in Rumania, south Russia and Asia, usually on the steppes.

Lesser Spotted Eagle, *Aquila pomarina,* 24-26 in. Breeds in east Europe and west Asia, and feeds for the greater part on frogs, worms and larvae.

Imperial Eagle, *Aquila heliaca,* 31-33 in. Breeds in the eastern Balkans and further eastwards right to China; there is a race of it in Spain.

Spotted Eagle, *Aquila clanga,* 26-29 in. Breeds in east Europe and further east in Asia to China.

Crowned Hawk-eagle, *Stephanoaetus coronatus,* 34 in. Found in tropical and south Africa, but rare. It lives in forests and feeds amongst other things on monkeys.

Verreaux's Eagle, *Aquila verreauxi,* 30 in. Found in mountain regions in East Africa.

(above) Long-crested Hawk-eagle; Bonelli's
Eagle; *(below)* Rufous-bellied Eagle

(above) Golden Eagle; Lesser Spotted Eagle; Tawny Eagle
(centre) Crowned Hawk-eagle; Imperial Eagle; Spotted Eagle
(below) Verreaux's Eagle; Harpy Eagle; Monkey-eating Eagle

(above) Palm-nut Vulture; King Vulture;
Lammergeyer; Griffon Vulture
(below) Egyptian Vulture; Ruppell's Vulture

Harpy Eagle, *Harpia harpyja,* 31-37 in.
Found from Mexico to tropical South
America, but not common. It feeds on
monkeys, sloths, and sometimes sheep.
Monkey-eating Eagle, *Pithecophaga jefferyi,* 33 in. Found on the Philippines
where it feeds principally on monkeys.

The *true vultures* are eagle-sized birds,
with naked or almost naked heads. They
feed on carrion and are found in the
tropical and subtropical regions of
Europe, Asia and Africa. Externally
they resemble the American vultures but
the two groups are not closely related.

Palm-nut Vulture, *Gypohierax angolensis,* 23 in. Found in Africa, where it
feeds on birds, fish and insects and also
on the nuts of the oil-palm.
King Vulture, *Sarcogyps calvus,* 31 in.
Found both in India and south-east
Asia.
Lammergeyer, *Gypaetus barbatus,* 40-45
in. A rare bird of the mountain regions
of southernmost Europe, and also found
in Asia and Africa. It flies high up with
the bones of carrion and lets them fall
and break against cliffs so that it can get
to the marrow. It breaks up tortoises
in the same way.
Griffon Vulture, *Gyps fulvus,* 38-41 in.
Breeds in parts of south Europe, west
Asia and Africa. In addition to carrion it
also takes insects.
Egyptian Vulture, *Neophron percnopterus,*
23-26 in. Breeds in south Europe, west
Asia and Africa. In addition to carrion
it takes rats, mice, lizards, birds' eggs and
grasshoppers.
Ruppell's Griffon, *Gyps ruppelli,* 41 in.
Found in Africa from Senegal to Somaliland.

Storks

THE STORKS, Ciconii, are large long-legged and long-necked birds with large beaks. They often have a web between the front toes. The food, which they find on the ground or in shallow water, is exclusively animal and consists largely of amphibians and fish. There are six groups: the ibises, the true storks, the spoonbills, the Hammerkop, the herons and the flamingos.

Ibises

The ibises, Threskiornithidae, consist of some 30 species. They are sociable birds which often breed in large colonies in trees, on cliffs or on the ground; they fly with outstretched neck.

White-faced Ibis, *Plegadis chihi*, 18-21 in. Found in North and South America, usually near to lakes and marshes.
Glossy Ibis, *Plegadis falcinellus*, 22 in. Found in a small area of Italy, in northeast Balkans, west and south Asia, Australia, and in America from U.S.A. to Argentina. Often lives in large flocks in marshes, where it hunts for aquatic animals; it also takes grasshoppers and other insects.
Sacred Ibis, *Threskiornis aethiopicus*, 15½ in. Found in Africa south of the Sahara, in Madagascar and Arabia. It was at one time found in Egypt where it was worshipped and even embalmed.
Scarlet Ibis, *Guara rubra*, 23 in. Found in tropical South America. This and the white ibis are so similar that many authorities maintain that they are only colour variations of the same species.
White Ibis, *Guara alba*, 23 in. Found in south-east United States, Mexico and central America.

(from above) White-faced Ibis; Glossy Ibis; Sacred Ibis; Scarlet Ibis; White Ibis; Waldrapp

(*from above*) Black-faced Ibis; Bare-fronted
Whispering Ibis; Straw-necked Ibis;
Spoonbill; African Spoonbill;
Royal Spoonbill; Roseate Spoonbill

Waldrapp, *Geronticus eremita,* 27 in.
Found locally in south-west Asia and
north-east Africa.
Black-faced Ibis, *Theristicus melanopis,*
27 in. Found in South America.
Bare-fronted Whispering Ibis, *Phimo-
sus infuscatus,* 19½ in. Found in South
America.
Straw-necked Ibis, *Carphibis spinicollis,*
32 in. Found in south Australia; it takes
many injurious insects and larvae.
Spoonbill, *Platalea leucorodia,* 34 in.
Breeds in the Balkans, south Spain,
Holland, as well as in Asia from Asia
Minor to China, and in Somaliland. It
lives in marshes and estuaries and feeds
on small animals in shallow water.
African Spoonbill, *Platalea alba,* 33 in.
Found in Africa south of the Sahara.
Royal Spoonbill, *Platalea regia,* 31 in.
Found in Australia, New Guinea and
parts of Indonesia.
Roseate Spoonbill, *Ajaja ajaja,* 27-31 in.
Found in North and South America;
only the old birds have a naked head.

Storks

The true storks, Ciconiidae, are large
birds with long legs. They are mute as
adults and can only clatter with the bill.
They fly with outstretched neck and
backwardly directed legs.

Black Stork, *Ciconia nigra,* 38 in. Breeds
in East Europe and further eastwards
in Asia to China. They feed on small fish,
frogs and aquatic insects and build their
nests in deciduous trees.
Abdim's Stork, *Sphenorhynchus abdimi,*
25 in. Found in Africa south of the
Sahara. It breeds in colonies in trees.
Maguari Stork, *Euxenura galeata,* 43 in.
Found in South America.

Wood Ibis, *Mycteria americana,* 43 in. Found from southern United States to South America.

White Stork, *Ciconia ciconia,* 40 in. Breeds in large areas of Europe northwards to Denmark, in Spain and in north Asia and north Africa. The European individuals winter in south Africa. Storks feed mainly on earthworms and beetles, but also take frogs, snakes and lizards. They originally nested in colonies in high woodland trees but now often build on roofs.

Open-bill, *Anastomus lamelligerus,* 28 in. Found in central Africa. It feeds on fish and freshwater molluscs.

Painted Stork, *Ibis leucocephalus,* 39 in. Found in India, Ceylon and south-east Asia, often breeding in colonies in trees in the middle of villages.

Marabou Stork, *Leptoptilos crumeniferus,* 48 in. Found in Africa south of the Sahara. It breeds in colonies in trees and feeds mostly on carrion. The naked

(above) Black Stork; Abdim's Stork; Maguari Stork; Wood Ibis
(centre) White Stork; Open-bill; *(below)* Painted Stork; Marabou Stork

(above) Jabiru; Black-necked Stork
(below) Saddle-bill Stork

Shoebills

Shoebill, *Balaeniceps rex*, 58 in. Found in Sudan, Uganda and parts of the Congo, this is the only species in the family Balaenicipitidae. When it flies it bends the neck and rests the heavy head with its colossal bill on the shoulders. It is not a good flier, and as a rule it flies low. The male is somewhat larger than the female. Shoebills feed on young crocodiles, small terrapins, frogs and fish, and the characteristic bill is probably adapted for getting lungfish and terrapins out of the mud at the bottom of rivers. It builds a nest in swamps on a 3 ft.-high pile of grass turfs and water plants.

Hammerkop

Hammerkop, *Scopus umbretta*, 23 in. Found in Africa south of the Sahara, in Arabia and Madagascar, this is the only species in the family Scopidae. In flight it holds the neck almost straight out and the feet straight back. It lives along the rivers and in swamps and feeds mostly on fish and other aquatic animals. The relatively large nest is often built in a cleft branch low over the ground. The natives say that the nest consists of three rooms, a front room for observation, a living room for the young and a bedroom, where the eggs are incubated.

throat pouch is air-filled and connected with the nostrils.

Jabiru, *Jabiru mycteria*, 58 in. Found from Mexico to Argentina. It hunts for food in muddy flood water.

Black-necked Stork, *Xenorhynchus asiaticus*, 50 in. Found in the area from southern Asia to Australia.

Saddle-bill Stork, *Ephippiorhynchus senegalensis*, 58 in. Found in Africa south of the Sahara. It lives mostly along the rivers and breeds in high trees.

Herons

The herons, Ardeidae, are large birds with long broad wings and a slow wing-beat. In flight the long neck is held in an S, and the head rests between the shoulders. They are found over the whole of the earth except in the polar regions, feed mostly on fish and aquatic animals and breed in colonies.

(from above) Shoebill; Hammerkop

Great White Heron, *Egretta alba,* 35 in. Breeds in the Balkans east into Asia, in Africa and from the southern United States to South America. The ornamental plumes of this and the next species were formerly much used in millinery.

Little Egret, *Egretta garzetta,* 22 in. Breeds in south Europe, as well as in Africa, Madagascar, central and south Asia and southwards to Australia.

Heron, *Ardea cinerea,* 36 in. Breeds throughout Europe except in the northeast and south-west, as well as in large parts of Asia and Africa. Feeds mostly on small fish, frogs and crustaceans, which it hunts in lakes, marshes and along the sea coast. It breeds in colonies in high trees.

Black-headed Heron, *Ardea melanocephala,* 35 in. Common on the lakes and rivers of tropical Africa.

Little Blue Heron, *Florida caerulea,* 22 in. Found in both north and south America.

Louisiana Heron, *Hydranassa tricolor,* 21-25 in. Found in North America south to northern South America.

Purple Heron, *Ardea purpurea,* 31 in. Breeds in Holland, south Europe, the whole of Africa and in south and east Asia. It builds in reeds or low bushes.

Squacco Heron, *Ardeola ralloides,* 18 in. Breeds in south Spain, the Balkans, west Asia, Africa and Madagascar. It nests in reed thickets along the edges of rivers and lakes.

Cattle Egret, *Ardeola ibis,* 20 in. Breeds in south Portugal, south Spain, Africa, Asia and South America. It usually lives near to cattle, where it catches insects.

Reef Egret, *Demigretta sacra,* 21½ in. Found in Australia, New Zealand, Indonesia and south-east Asia.

(above, from left) Great White Heron; Heron
(below) Little Egret

133

(*above*) Black-headed Heron; Little Blue Heron; Louisiana Heron
(*below*) Purple Heron; Squacco Heron; Cattle Egret

Yellow-crowned Night Heron, *Nyctianassa violacea*, 19-22 in. Found from southern United States to South America.
Little Bittern, *Ixobrychus minutus*, 14 in. Breeds in central and south Europe, Africa, Asia and America. It lives sheltered among high grass and reeds.
Night Heron, *Nycticorax nycticorax*, 24 in. Breeds in south Europe, Asia, Africa and America. It hunts at twilight.

New Guinea Bittern, *Zonerodius heliosylus*, 29 in. Found in New Guinea and the Aru Islands in swamps and along rivers.
Bittern, *Botaurus stellaris*, 30 in. Breeds in Europe, except in the north, and in north Africa and Asia. It seldom comes out of the reed thickets during the day. The male makes a deep booming sound, mostly heard at night.

(*above*) Reef Egret; Yellow-crowned Night Heron; Little Bittern
(*below*) Night Heron; New Guinea Bittern; Bittern

bill, which they hold upside down with the lower bill uppermost, the neck being held straight downwards. The nest is a mud cone about 18 in. high.

Greater Flamingo, *Phoenicopterus ruber roseus,* 60 in. Found in South Spain, the Rhone delta and in large parts of Africa and Asia.
Chilean Flamingo, *Phoenicopterus ruber chilensis,* 42 in. Found in temperate South America.
Rosy Flamingo, *Phoenicopterus ruber ruber,* 56 in. Widespread from the West Indies to northern South America, and in Galapagos.
Lesser Flamingo, *Phoeniconaias minor,* 36 in. Found in Africa, Madagascar and north-west India.

(from above) <u>Black Bittern</u>; Banded
Tiger-heron; Boat-billed Heron

Black Bittern, *Dupetor flavicollis,* 22 in. Found from South Asia to Australia.
Banded Tiger-Heron, *Tigrisoma lineatum,* 29 in. Found in Mexico and central America.
Boat-billed Heron, *Cochlearius cochlearius,* 19 in. Found from Mexico to south Brazil. It resembles the shoebill, but is most closely related to the night herons.

Flamingos

The flamingos, Phoenicopteridae, have long necks and long legs. The bill is bent at an angle in the middle, and the edges of the lower bill cover those of the upper bill. Flamingos live in large flocks in shallow water and lagoons. They collect small water animals and algae by sieving the water through the

(above) Greater Flamingo
(centre) Chilean Flamingo; Rosy Flamingo
(below) Lesser Flamingo

(from above) Red-billed Tropic-bird;
Red-tailed Tropic-bird;
White-tailed Tropic-bird

Tropic-birds

The tropic-birds, Phaethontidae, contain only 3 species. The wings are long, and the tail is wedge-shaped with the two central feathers greatly elongated and very narrow. Tropic-birds can hover motionless and then dive from great heights for fish and squid. They are found in tropical oceans. The clutch consists of only one egg, which is laid on a cliff ledge or on the ground.

Red-billed Tropic-bird, *Phaeton aethereus,* 25-39 in. Found in the Atlantic, Pacific and Indian Oceans.
Red-tailed Tropic-bird, *Phaeton rubricaudus,* 38 in. Found in the Pacific and Indian Oceans.
White-tailed Tropic-bird, *Phaeton lepturus,* 33 in. Found in the Atlantic, Pacific and Indian Oceans.

Pelicans

THE PELICANS and their relatives, Pelecaniformes, are large swimming birds, in which the feet are webbed not only between the four front toes but also between the second toe and the inwardly directed back toe. The bill is long and powerful and the plumage is thick and strong. They mostly live out at sea, but some are also found on large lakes and along rivers.

The group contains the tropic-birds, the pelicans, the gannets, the cormorants, the darters, and the frigate-birds.

(above) Pink-backed Pelican
(below) White Pelican

Pelicans

The true pelicans, Pelecanidae, consist of 8 species. They are found in large flocks in the tropics and subtropics. The beak is 18 in. long and the skin between the two branches of the lower mandible can be enlarged into a pocket with the upper beak forming a long narrow roof. In spite of their size the pelicans sit high on the water because their bones are full of air and the air sacs in the body are large.

Pink-backed Pelican, *Pelecanus rufescens,* 55 in. Found in Africa south of the Sahara and in Madagascar.
White Pelican, *Pelecanus onocrotalus,* 54-70 in. Found along the rivers and lakes from Rumania and Bulgaria in the north to equatorial Africa in the south and north India to the east. The male is larger than the female.

Spot-billed Pelican, *Pelecanus philippinensis,* 50-59 in. Found in south Asia from India to the Philippines.
Brown Pelican, *Pelecanus occidentalis,* 39-52 in. Found from the southern coastal regions of west Canada to southern South America, and in the West Indies. It fishes exclusively in salt water and can dive from a height of more than 60 ft. Air sacs in the breast region act as shock absorbers against the water surface.
Australian Pelican, *Pelecanus conspicillatus,* 59-63 in. Found in Australia and New Guinea.
Rough-billed Pelican, *Pelecanus erythrorhynchus,* 52-67 in. Widespread in north and central America. In the breeding season it has a horny growth on the upper side of the bill, which disappears when the breeding time is finished.
Crested Pelican, *Pelecanus crispus,* 59-70 in. Found in the Balkans, north Africa and east through Asia to China.

(*above*) Spot-billed Pelican; Brown Pelican; Australian Pelican
(*below*) Rough-billed Pelican; Crested Pelican

(*from above*) Blue-faced Booby;
Brown Booby; Blue-footed Booby;
Variegated Booby; Cape Gannet; Gannet

Gannets

The gannets, Sulidae, consist of 9 large species, all rather similar in appearance and habits. The bill is long, powerful and pointed and the wings are long and pointed. Gannets only come to land to breed, which they do in large colonies. They can dive from heights of 100 ft., higher than any other bird. They have small elastic air sacs under the skin which take up the shock when they hit the water.

Blue-faced Booby, *Sula dactylatra,* 31-36 in. Found in tropical seas.
Brown Booby, *Sula leucogaster,* 32 in. Breeds on small islands in all tropical seas.
Blue-footed Booby, *Sula nebouxii,* 34 in. Breeds along the Pacific coasts from Mexico to Peru.
Variegated Booby, *Sula variegata,* 24½ in. Found off the west coast of South America, where it is a most important guano producer in Peru and Chile.
Cape Gannet, *Sula capensis,* 26-30 in. Breeds along the coasts of South Africa.
Gannet, *Sula bassana,* 36 in. Breeds on small islands off Britain, Faeroes, Iceland, Brittany, Norway, Newfoundland and in the Gulf of St. Lawrence. In all there are only 20 to 30 colonies with a total of 80-90,000 breeding pairs. The gannet lays only one egg in the clutch and the mottled-brown juvenile gets its white plumage when it is about 3 years old.

Cormorants

The cormorants, Phalacrocoracidae, consist of about 30 species. They have a long bill, which ends in a sharp hook, a long neck and a rounded tail with stiff

(*above*) Bougainville's Shag; Spotted Shag; Shag; Pelagic Cormorant
(*below*) Gaimard's Cormorant; Pied Cormorant; Cormorant

feathers. They are principally coastal birds, but some live on lakes and rivers. They feed on herring, eels, blennies and other fish and may also damage fisheries. They dive from the water surface and can reach quite far down. In China and Japan trained cormorants are used for catching fish. Their loose plumage easily absorbs water, and one often sees them sitting with stretched wings held out to dry. Cormorants nest in colonies, some in trees, others on cliff ledges or on the ground.

Bougainville's Shag, *Phalacrocorax bougainvillii,* 29 in. Breeds on islands off the coast of Peru and Chile and is by far the most important guano-producing bird. It is in fact said to be the world's most useful wild bird, and thousands of tons of guano are collected yearly for manure. It appears that this species annually fishes ten times as many tons of fish as the local fishermen.

Spotted Shag, *Phalacrocorax punctatus,* 23 in. Found along the coast of New Zealand.

Shag, *Phalacrocorax aristotelis,* 30 in. Breeds along the coasts of Iceland, Norway, Britain, and in many places along the rocky coasts of west Europe and the Mediterranean.

(*above*) Long-tailed Cormorant; Bank
Cormorant; (*below*) Flightless Cormorant

Pelagic Cormorant, *Phalacrocorax pelagicus,* 25-29 in. Found in the Bering Sea
and the north Pacific.
Gaimard's Cormorant, *Phalacrocorax
gaimardi,* 27 in. Found along the coasts
of Peru, Chile and Patagonia.
Pied Cormorant, *Phalacrocorax varius,*
35 in. Common in the waters around
Australia and New Zealand.
Cormorant, *Phalacrocorax carbo,* 36 in.
Breeds in coastal areas and on lakes, in
north-east America, Greenland, Iceland
and Europe to South Asia, Australia
and New Zealand, as well as in Africa.
Long-tailed Cormorant, *Phalacrocorax
africanus,* 21-23 in. Found on the lakes
of Africa from Gambia and Egypt
southwards.

Bank Cormorant, *Phalacrocorax neglec-
tus,* 26-29 in. Found along the coasts of
South Africa.
Flightless Cormorant, *Nannopterum
harrisi,* 36 in. Found only on the
Galapagos Islands. It has very small
wings and cannot fly.

Darters

The darters, Anhingidae, with four
species, are all very similar apart from
colour. They have a long pointed beak,
a small head and a proportionately long
and thin neck. They often fish together
in large flocks, harpooning the fish with
the beak. They live on rivers, lakes and
marshes and build nests in the neighbouring trees.

(*above*) American Darter
(*below*) African Darter

(*above*) Lesser Frigate-bird; Christmas Frigate bird
(*below*) Great Frigate-bird; Magnificent Frigate bird

American Darter, *Anhinga anhinga,*
27-35 in. Widespread from southern
U.S.A. to Argentina.
African Darter, *Anhinga rufa,* 35 in.
Found in Iraq, Madagascar, and Africa
south of the Sahara.

Frigate-birds

In the frigate-birds, Fregatidae, the
wings are proportionately longer than
in other birds. They are the fastest and
most dexterous fliers of all sea birds.
They have a web between the toes and
were probably originally swimming
birds. They live mostly out at sea and
can hover for hours at a time, without
apparent exertion. Frigate-birds feed
on flying fish, but also get food by
chasing gannets, cormorants, gulls and
other birds and making them disgorge
their prey; in addition they spy out prey
from the air, dive down to within a few

inches of the surface and snap up
fish, squid and carrion. They breed in
large colonies in the tops of bushes and
small trees, often in company with
other sea birds, and with the nests close
together. During the breeding season
the male develops a large naked red
throat sac, which can be inflated. The
females are significantly larger than the
males.

Lesser Frigate-bird, *Fregata ariel,* 30 in.
Breeds on islands in all three oceans.
Christmas Frigate-bird, *Fregata an-
drewsi,* 30-39 in. Breeds only on a few
islands in the Indian Ocean.
Great Frigate-bird, *Fregata minor,* 34-39
in. Found in the tropical parts of all
three oceans.
Magnificent Frigate-bird, *Fregata mag-
nificens,* 36-39 in. Distributed along the
tropical Atlantic and Pacific coasts of
America. It sometimes visits Bermuda,
Florida and south California. This is the
species which is known to sailors as the
man-o'-war bird.

Swans, Geese and Ducks

THE ORDER ANSERIFORMES contains the familiar ducks, swans and geese, and in addition the screamers of South America.

Screamers

The screamers, Anhimidae, contain three South American species. They have almost no web on the feet but are still able to swim well. There are two pointed horny spurs on the edge of each wing, which are used as weapons.

Horned Screamer

(from above) Derbian Screamer; Crested Screamer

Derbian Screamer, *Chauna chavaria,* 33 in. Found in north Colombia and Venezuela.
Crested Screamer, *Chauna torquata,* 33 in. Found in southern South America.
Horned Screamer, *Anhima cornuta,* 26 in. Found in northern South America. It has a long 'horn' on the forehead.

True Ducks and Geese

The family Anatidae contains a large number of species widely distributed, particularly in the northern hemisphere, often living in large flocks. The group may be divided into two subfamilies: the goose-like Anserinae, in which the plumage is practically the same in both sexes and courtship ceremonies are not spectacular—the swans, geese and tree ducks, and the duck-like Anatinae, in which the plumage of the sexes is usually different and the courtship dances are complicated.

The *swans* are very large birds with long necks and broad wings. They feed on

(above) Mute Swan; Whooper Swan; Black Swan
(below) Coscoroba Swan; Black-necked Swan; Whistling Swan; Trumpeter Swan

aquatic plants and small animals, and all except the next species can trumpet.

Mute Swan, *Cygnus olor,* 60 in. Breeds in Britain, Denmark, south Sweden, Germany, the Baltic countries and large parts of north and central Asia.

Whooper Swan, *Cygnus cygnus,* 60 in. Breeds in Iceland, Lapland, Russia and north Asia and migrates southwards in winter to Britain and Scandinavia.

Black Swan, *Cygnus atratus,* 46 in. Found in Australia and Tasmania.

Coscoroba Swan, *Coscoroba coscoroba,* 35 in. Found in southern South America.

Black-necked Swan, *Cygnus melanocoryphus,* 39 in. Found in southern South America and the Falkland Islands.

Whistling Swan, *Cygnus columbianus,* 47 in. Breeds in Arctic Canada and winters to the south.

Trumpeter Swan, *Cygnus cygnus buccinator,* 60 in. A rare North American form of the Whooper Swan.

The *geese* have short powerful bills with broad beak nails. They feed mostly on grass.

Western Bean Goose, *Anser fabalis fabalis,* 28-35 in. Breeds in north Scandinavia and north Russia, and winters in west and south Europe.

Pink-footed Goose, *Anser fabalis brachyrhynchus,* 24-30 in. Breeds in Greenland, Iceland, and Spitsbergen.

Emperor Goose, *Anser canagicus,* 30 in. Breeds in Alaska and north-east Siberia.

White-fronted Goose, *Anser albifrons,* 26-30 in. Breeds in Arctic north America, Greenland, Kola peninsula and north Siberia.

(above) Western Bean Goose; Pink-footed Goose; Emperor Goose
(centre) White-fronted Goose; Swan Goose; *(below)* Grey Lag Goose; Snow Goose

Swan Goose, *Anser cygnoides,* 36 in. Breeds in northern Siberia; domesticated as the Chinese Goose.

Grey Lag Goose, *Anser anser,* 30-35 in. Breeds in Iceland, Scotland, Scandinavia, east Europe and central Asia. This is the original form of the domesticated goose.

Snow Goose, *Anser caerulescens,* 25-30 in. Breeds in Arctic North America and north Greenland. There is a white phase as well as the blue form shown.

Hawaiian Goose, *Branta sandvicensis,* 23 in. Found on the volcanic slopes of Hawaii, where only about 50 specimens now remain; in addition some are kept and bred in captivity.

Brent Goose, *Branta bernicla,* 22-24 in. Breeds in Arctic north America, north Greenland, north Siberia and Spitsbergen, and winters in Britain, Denmark and on the coasts of west Europe and America.

Barnacle Goose, *Branta leucopsis,* 23-27 in. Breeds in Greenland, Spitsbergen and Novaya Zemlya, and winters in Ireland, Scotland, Holland and Holstein.

Canada Goose, *Branta canadensis,* 36-40 in. Breeds in northern North America; introduced into Europe.

Red-breasted Goose, *Branta ruficollis,* 21-22 in. Breeds in west Siberia and winters in west Asia and sometimes in Europe.

Bar-headed Goose, *Anser indicus,* 29 in. Breeds in central Asia.

The *tree-ducks* have proportionately long legs and large feet; they often sit in trees.

White-faced Tree-duck, *Dendrocygna viduata,* 15 in. Found in the tropics of Africa and South America.

Red-billed Tree-duck, *Dendrocygna autumnalis,* 20 in. Found in central and south America.

(above) Hawaiian Goose; Brent Goose; Barnacle Goose
(below) Canada Goose; Red-breasted Goose; Bar-headed Goose

The duck-like *Anatinae* may be divided into six groups. The majority live on fresh water and feed on aquatic plants, snails and larvae, but there are a few which are goose-like in appearance and which usually graze on land. In addition to the dabbling ducks, such as mallard, teal and gadwall, there are the perching ducks which nest in tree holes, the eiders, the shelducks and the sea ducks, which include the scoters, golden-eyes and mergansers. The latter have a long thin bill and feed on fish.

European Wigeon, *Anas penelope,* 18 in. Breeds in Iceland, Scotland, Scandinavia, north-east Europe and north Asia.

Pintail, *Anas acuta,* 22 in. Its breeding range is almost the same as that of the wigeon, but it is also found in North America.

Philippine Duck, *Anas luzonica,* 19-23 in. Found on lakes and meadows in the Philippines.

Gadwall, *Anas strepera,* 20 in. Breeds in Iceland, Britain, and many places in

White-faced Tree-duck; Red-billed Tree-duck

(from above) European Wigeon; <u>Pintail;</u>
Philippine Duck; Gadwall; Yellow-billed Duck;
Mallard; <u>Garganey;</u> Teal; Shoveler

Europe, as well as in north Asia and north America.

Yellow-billed Duck, *Anas undulata*, 21½ in. Found in Africa from Uganda and Kenya to the Cape.

Mallard, *Anas platyrhynchos*, 23 in. Widely distributed almost everywhere in the temperate belt of the northern hemisphere, and also common in the southern Arctic. Domesticated ducks are derived from this species.

Garganey, *Anas querquedula,* 15 in. Breeds in south Scandinavia, west and central Europe and north Asia.

Teal, *Anas crecca*, 14 in. Breeds in north and central Europe, north Asia and large parts of north America.

Shoveler, *Anas clypeata*, 20 in. Breeds in large areas of north and central Europe and north Asia and in the western parts of north America.

Maned Wood Duck, *Chenonetta jubata*, 21½ in. Found in Australia. This and the following five species belong among the wood ducks.

Carolina Wood Duck, *Aix sponsa*, 17½ in. Breeds in the temperate regions of North America.

Brazilian Teal, *Amazonetta brasiliensis*, 15½ in. Found in eastern South America.

Comb Duck, *Sarkidiornis melanota*, 25½-29½ in. Found in Africa south of the Sahara, in India and south-east Asia.

Mandarin Duck, *Aix galericulata*, 16½ in. Found in east Asia. The male is easily known by the erect wing fan.

Spur-winged Goose, *Plectropterus gambensis*, 35-39 in. Found in Africa south of the Sahara. It has powerful spurs on the edges of the wings.

Radjah Shelduck, *Tadorna radjah*, 25½ in. Breeds in north Australia, New Guinea and the Moluccas.

Ruddy Shelduck, *Tadorna ferruginea*, 25 in. Breeds in north Africa, south Spain, south Balkans and in Asia eastwards to China.

(above) Maned Wood Duck; Carolina Wood Duck; Brazilian Teal
(below) Comb Duck; Mandarin Duck; Spur-winged Goose

South American Crested Duck, *Lophonetta specularioides*, 23½ in. Found in the southern parts of South America.

Egyptian Goose, *Alopochen aegyptiacus*, 27½ in. Breeds in Africa south of the Sahara and along the Nile.

Australian Shelduck, *Tadorna tadornoides*, 28½ in. Found in south Australia and Tasmania.

Shelduck, *Tadorna tadorna*, 24 in. Breeds along the coasts of north Europe and in Asia eastwards to Tibet and Mongolia. It digs holes in banks and slopes and may also nest in rabbit burrows, even if these have not been deserted by their owners.

Andean Goose, *Chloephaga melanoptera*, 27 in. Found up to 10,000 ft. in the Andes.

(above) Radjah Shelduck; Ruddy Shelduck; South American Crested Duck
(below) Egyptian Goose; Australian Shelduck; Shelduck

(above) Andean Goose; Ashy-headed Goose; Blue-winged Goose; Orinoco Goose
(below) Magellan Goose, male and female; Lesser Kelp Goose, male and female

Ashy-headed Goose, *Chloephaga poliocephala,* 22 in. Found in southern South America.
Blue-winged Goose, *Cyanochen cyanopterus,* 23 in. Found high up in the mountains of Abyssinia.
Orinoco Goose, *Neochen jubatus,* 25 in. Found in northern South America.
Magellan Goose, *Chloephaga picta,* 23 in. Found in southern South America and the Falkland Islands.
Lesser Kelp Goose, *Chloephaga hybrida hybrida,* 23 in. Found on the cliff coasts in southernmost South America and the Falkland Islands.
Australian Magpie Goose, *Anseranas semipalmata,* 48 in. Found in Australia and south New Guinea.
Cape Barren Goose, *Cereopsis novaehollandiae,* 39 in. Breeds on islands off south Australia, and is now rare.
Falkland Flightless Steamer Duck, *Tachyeres brachypterus,* 27 in. Found on the Falkland Islands. Although unable to fly it moves fast on the water, rather like a paddle steamer.
Flying Steamer Duck, *Tachyeres patachonicus,* 27 in. Found in southern South America.

(from left) Australian Magpie Goose;
Cape Barren Goose

Red-crested Pochard, *Netta rufina*, 22 in. Breeds in Holland, Denmark, north Germany, south Europe, west Africa and west Asia. Mainly found on freshwater lakes.

Tufted Duck, *Aythya fuligula*, 17 in. Breeds in north Europe and eastwards through north Asia to Kamtchatka, and winters in west Europe. It dives to the bottom of lakes for bivalve molluscs.

Ferruginous Duck, *Aythya nyroca*, 16 in. Breeds in south and east Europe, north Africa and central Asia.

Scaup, *Aythya marila*, 19 in. Breeds in Iceland, Scandinavia and the Arctic regions of Siberia and north America.

Pochard, *Aythya ferina*, 18 in. Breeds in Europe from Britain eastwards into Asia. It is found in lakes and marshes and along the coasts.

Canvas-back, *Aythya valisineria*, 18-21 in. Breeds in North America where it is a popular game bird.

(left) Falkland Flightless Steamer Duck
(right) Flying Steamer Duck

Long-tailed Duck, *Clangula hyemalis*, male 21 in., female 16 in. Breeds in the Arctic and winters in north Europe. It feeds largely on snails and bivalves.

Harlequin Duck, *Histrionicus histrionicus*, 17 in. Breeds in Arctic north America, Greenland, Iceland and Siberia, and lives near rivers and waterfalls.

(above) Red-crested Pochard; Tufted Duck; Ferruginous Duck
(below) Scaup; Pochard; Canvas-back

(above) Long-tailed Duck; Harlequin Duck; *(centre)* Velvet Scoter; Common
Scoter; Surf Scoter; *(below)* King Eider; Eider; Steller's Eider

Velvet Scoter, *Melanitta fusca,* 22 in.
Breeds in the far north of Europe and
in Asia, and winters in northern parts
of Europe.

Common Scoter, *Melanitta nigra,* 19 in.
Breeds in northernmost Europe and Asia
(a few in north Britain), and winters
in north and west Europe. It lives
mostly near open water; the male is the
only completely black duck.

Surf Scoter, *Melanitta perspicillata,* 21 in.
Breeds only in northernmost north
America. Several specimens have strayed
from there to Europe.

King Eider, *Somateria spectabilis,* 22 in.
Breeds in the high Arctic; occasionally
seen in Europe in winter.

Eider, *Somateria mollissima,* 23 in. Breeds

along the coasts of Iceland, Scotland
and Scandinavia, as well as in Greenland
and northern North America. The nest
is lined with dark grey down which the
female plucks from her breast with
her bill.

Steller's Eider, *Polysticta stelleri,* 18 in.
Breeds along the coasts of Siberia and
west Alaska; occasionally strays to north
Europe.

Goldeneye, *Bucephala clangula,* 18 in.
Breeds in north-east Europe, north
Asia and northern North America. The
wings make a whistling sound, especially
when taking off from the water.

Barrow's Goldeneye, *Bucephala islan-
dica,* 21 in. Breeds in Greenland, Iceland
and parts of north-west America.

(above) Goldeneye; Barrow's Goldeneye; Red-breasted Merganser, male and female
(below) Hooded Merganser; Smew; Goosander

Red-breasted Merganser, *Mergus serrator*, 23 in. Breeds in northern North America, Greenland, north Europe and north Asia, often near the sea. It feeds on small fish, which it catches under water but swallows when it returns to the surface.

Hooded Merganser, *Mergus cucullatus*, 17 in. Breeds in wooded regions of North America from Alaska to Florida.

Smew, *Mergus albellus*, 16 in. Breeds in north-east Scandinavia, Russia and Siberia. It lives in fjords, bays and lakes.

Goosander, *Mergus merganser*, 26 in. Breeds in north America, north Europe, Switzerland and large parts of Asia. It nests in hollow trees or free on the ground.

Andean Torrent Duck, *Merganetta armata*, 14 in. Found on the fast streams of the Andes; it has a sharp spur on the wing.

White-headed Duck, *Oxyura leucocephala*, 18 in. Breeds in some of the Mediterranean countries and in west Asia, usually on inland lakes or brackish lagoons.

Andean Torrent Duck; White-headed Duck

(above) Magellan Diving-petrel
(below) Common Diving-petrel

Storm-petrels

The storm-petrels, Hydrobatidae, feed mainly on plankton at the surface of the sea, and nest among rocks on small islands.

Black-bellied Storm-petrel, *Fregetta tropica*, 7½ in. Found in the southerly parts of the world's oceans.
Leach's Storm-petrel, *Oceanodroma leucorhoa*, 8 in. Breeds on islands in the north Atlantic and Pacific.
Least Storm-Petrel, *Halocyptena microsoma*, 5½ in. Breeds only on San Benito Island, Lower California.

Petrels

THE PETRELS, Procellariiformes, contain over 100 species of oceanic birds, most of which are found in the southern hemisphere. In contrast to other birds the nostrils open out in horn-like tubes, which lie on top of the bill. The order is divided into 4 families: the diving-petrels, the storm-petrels, the true petrels and the albatrosses.

Diving-petrels

The diving-petrels, Pelecanoididae, are found distributed over great areas of the southern hemisphere.

Magellan Diving-petrel, *Pelecanoides magellani*, 7-8 in. Breeds on the coasts of southern South America.
Common Diving-petrel, *Pelecanoides urinatrix*, 7 in. Found throughout the sub-antarctic seas.

(from above) Black-bellied Storm-petrel; Leach's Storm-petrel; Least Storm-petrel; Wilson's Petrel; Storm-petrel; White-faced Storm-petrel

Wilson's Petrel, *Oceanites oceanicus,* 7 in. Breeds in the far south, but stragglers occasionally reach Europe.

Storm-petrel, *Hydrobates pelagicus,* 6 in. Breeds in Iceland, Faeroes, western Britain, the west coast of France and in the western Mediterranean.

White-faced Storm-petrel, *Pelagodroma marina,* 7¾ in. Found in tropical seas.

Petrels and Shearwaters

The true petrels, shearwaters and fulmars live almost everywhere in the seas of the world. They are wonderful fliers and gliders and can land on the water.

Bermuda Petrel, *Pterodroma cahow,* 13½ in. Once abundant in Bermuda, but thought to be extinct until recently rediscovered on small outlying skerries.

Cape Pigeon, *Daption capensis,* 13½ in. Breeds in Antarctica and on islands to the north.

Sooty Shearwater, *Puffinus griseus,* 16 in. Breeds in the south temperate Atlantic and Pacific and migrates north in winter.

Black-capped Petrel, *Pterodroma hasitata,* 15½ in. Found in the north Atlantic.

Brown Petrel, *Adamastor cinereus,* 17½ in. Found in the southern oceans.

White-chinned Petrel, *Procellaria aequinoctialis,* 21 in. Found in the southern oceans.

Fulmar, *Fulmarus glacialis,* 18½ in. Found in the Arctic and north Atlantic, and breeds, amongst other places, in Greenland, Iceland, Faeroes and Britain. It is the commonest bird out in the Atlantic, where it feeds to a considerable extent on fish offal from trawlers.

Giant Petrel, *Macronectes giganteus,* 32-35 in. Found in the southern hemisphere from the temperate zone to Antarctica. It occurs in a white and a dark-brown phase.

(from above) Bermuda Petrel; Cape Pigeon; Sooty Shearwater; Black-capped Petrel; Brown Petrel; White-chinned Petrel; Fulmar; Giant Petrel

(above) Black-footed Albatross; Wandering Albatross; Short-tailed Albatross
(below) Shy Albatross; Sooty Albatross; Waved Albatross

Albatrosses

The albatrosses, Diomedeidae, are about the size of a goose or swan, and are found from the Antarctic to the tropics. They live out at sea for months, sleeping on the waves, drinking sea water and feeding on squids and other marine animals.

Black-footed Albatross, *Diomedea nigripes*, 29 in. Breeds on Hawaii and other Pacific islands.

Wandering Albatross, *Diomedea exu-*

lans, 43-50 in., with a wing span of 11-12 ft.; it can hover for hours at a time.

Short-tailed Albatross, *Diomedea albatrus*, 37-50 in. Breeds on small islands south-east of Japan, but now almost extinct.

Shy Albatross, *Diomedea cauta*, 34-39 in. Found in southern temperate seas.

Sooty Albatross, *Phoebetria fusca*, 32 in. Breeds on Tristan da Cunha, Gough, St. Paul and Amsterdam Islands.

Waved Albatross, *Diomedea irrorata*, 34 in. Found off the west coast of South America.

Penguins

THE PENGUINS, Sphenisciformes, contain only one family with some 17 species. The body is clothed in densely packed feathers, the feet have a web and the short legs sit so far back that the bird stands erect. The wings are stiff flippers and although penguins cannot fly, they swim remarkably well with the flippers. On land they walk upright or lie down and paddle along the snow with the flippers, like a toboggan. Penguins are found exclusively in the southern hemisphere, some in Antarctica, the majority in sub-antarctic waters and a single species on the equator. They feed on fish, crustaceans and molluscs and some are able to fast for months.

Adelie Penguin, *Pygoscelis adeliae,* 27 in. Breeds on the coasts of the Antarctic, often in large colonies. 7-8 weeks after hatching the young collect in crèches of 20-200 individuals under the supervision of some adults.

Ringed Penguin, *Pygoscelis antarctica,* 28 in. Breeds on South Georgia and neighbouring islands.

Galapagos Penguin, *Spheniscus mendiculus,* 19 in. Found only on the coasts of the Galapagos Islands.

Gentoo Penguin, *Pygoscelis papua,* 29 in. Breeds on the Falkland Islands, South Georgia and further southwards.

Rockhopper Penguin, *Eudyptes cristatus,* 27 in. Breeds on many sub-antarctic islands. It hops with the legs together.

Royal Penguin, *Eudyptes schlegeli,* 25-29 in. Found south of New Zealand.

Big-crested Penguin, *Eudyptes sclateri,* 27 in. Found south of New Zealand.

Yellow-eyed Penguin, *Megadyptes antipodes,* 29-31 in. Found on South Island, New Zealand.

(from above) Adelie Penguin; Ringed Penguin; Galapagos Penguin; Gentoo Penguin; Rockhopper Penguin; Royal Penguin; Big-crested Penguin; Yellow-eyed Penguin; Jackass Penguin; Magellan Penguin

(above) Emperor Penguin; King Penguin
(below) Little Penguin

Jackass Penguin, *Spheniscus demersus,* 23 in. Breeds in enormous colonies on small islands off the coast of South Africa, and sometimes occurs northwards to Angola and Natal.
Magellan Penguin, *Spheniscus magellanicus,* 27 in. Breeds on the coast of south Chile, Tierra del Fuego and the Falklands.
Emperor Penguin, *Aptenodytes forsteri,* 54 in. This is the largest and most southern of the penguins and breeds around the pole in the Antarctic; only four breeding places are known. During incubation the egg is held on the feet, covered by loose skin. The parents take turns to incubate whilst standing.
King Penguin, *Aptenodytes patagonica,* 40 in. Breeds on the coasts of South Georgia, Kerguelen and other islands.
Little Penguin, *Eudyptula minor,* 15 in. Common in Australian waters.

Grebes

THE GREBES, Podicipitiformes, form a small group of aquatic birds distributed over most of the earth except the Arctic and Antarctic. The plumage is very close, and grebes have more feathers than other birds. They fly poorly but dive very well, and feed on small fish, aquatic insects, crustaceans and pieces of plant.

Little Grebe, *Podiceps ruficollis,* 10½ in. Breeds in Europe from south Scandinavia southwards, and in Africa, Asia and Australia.
Slavonian Grebe, *Podiceps auritus,* 13 in. Breeds in northernmost Europe and America, also in Iceland.
Red-necked Grebe, *Podiceps grisegena,*

(above) Little Grebe
(centre) Slavonian Grebe
(below) Red-necked Grebe; Great Crested Grebe

17 in. Breeds from Denmark eastwards through Russia to North America.

Great Crested Grebe, *Podiceps cristatus,* 19 in. Found nearly everywhere in Europe except in the far north, as well as in Africa, Asia and Australia. In breeding dress the adult has elongated crest feathers and a collar of dark feathers.

Western Grebe, *Aechmophorus occidentalis,* 27 in. Breeds in western North America.

Hoary-headed Dabchick, *Podiceps poliocephalus,* 11½ in. Found in Australia and Tasmania.

Pied-billed Grebe, *Podilymbus podiceps,* 12 in. Found on small lakes in North America up to heights of 6,000 ft.

Black-necked Grebe, *Proctopus caspicus,* 11½ in. Breeds in Europe and Asia, with races in Africa and North America.

(from above) Great Northern Diver; Black-throated Diver; Red-throated Diver

(above) Western Grebe
(centre) Hoary-headed Dabchick
(below) Pied-billed Grebe; Black-necked Grebe

Divers

THE DIVERS, Gaviiformes, form a very small group with only four species distributed in the colder regions of the northern hemisphere. They fly, swim and dive well, but the feet are placed so far back that they are helpless on land. They feed on fish, crustaceans and bivalve molluscs.

Great Northern Diver, *Colymbus immer,* 27-32 in. Breeds in Alaska, north Canada, Greenland and Iceland.

Black-throated Diver, *Colymbus arcticus,* 23-27 in. Breeds in the far north of Europe, Asia and northern America.

Red-throated Diver, *Colymbus stellatus,* 21-24 in. Breeds around the Arctic and southwards to Scotland and Scandinavia.

Waders and Gulls

THE WADERS AND GULLS, Charadriiformes, are a large group of birds
adapted for life at sea, on the coasts, on
lakes and on open land. They include
the auks, stone curlews, crab plovers,
pratincoles, sheathbills, true plovers,
gulls and skuas. Some authorities place
the jacanas (p. 176) in this order.

Auks

The auks, Alcidae, are marine birds
with their centre of distribution in the
Arctic, although several species reach
southwards to California, west Europe
and Japan.

(from above) Tufted Puffin; Puffin;
Little Auk; Black Guillemot

(above) Razorbill
(centre) Guillemot
(below) Brünnich's Guillemot

Razorbill, *Alca torda,* 16 in. Breeds
along the coasts of the North Atlantic
and southwards to north France and
Denmark.
Guillemot, *Uria aalge,* 16½ in. Found
over nearly the whole of the northern
Atlantic and Pacific. It breeds on cliff
ledges in large colonies. The large pear-
shaped egg varies more in colour than
that of any other bird.
Brünnich's Guillemot, *Uria lomvia,*
16½ in. Breeds in the Arctic, including
Iceland.
Tufted Puffin, *Lunda cirrhata,* 15½ in.
Found in the Bering Sea and the North
Pacific.
Puffin, *Fratercula arctica,* 12 in. Breeds
along the coasts of the Arctic Ocean from
Greenland and eastwards to Novaya
Zemlya, and along the coasts of Iceland,
Faeroes, Britain and Norway. It digs its
nest hole under turf on cliffs. In winter

Stone Curlews

The stone curlews, Burhinidae, with some 9 species, are found principally in the tropics and are lacking in North America. They feed on mice, lizards, insects, larvae and worms.

Beach Stone Curlew, *Orthorhamphus magnirostris,* 22½ in. Found along the sea coasts in south-east Asia and Australia.
Spotted Thicknee, *Burhinus capensis,* 17 in. Found in many parts of Africa.
Stone Curlew, *Burhinus oedicnemus,* 16 in. Widely distributed in central and south Europe, north Africa and south Asia, living on steppes, heathland and meadows.

(from above) Least Auklet; Parrakeet Auklet; Crested Auklet

the colours of the beak disappear, and the beak becomes smaller, because the outermost horny layer is moulted.
Little Auk, *Plautus alle,* 8 in. Breeds in large colonies along the coasts of the Arctic Ocean and Greenland and eastwards to Novaya Zemlya as well as in north Iceland.
Black Guillemot, *Uria grylle,* 13½ in. Breeds in small colonies from the Arctic regions to north Europe. It nests in holes, in cliff crevices or under large boulders.
Least Auklet, *Aethia pusilla,* 10¼ in. Found in the Bering Sea and in the northern parts of the Pacific.
Parrakeet Auklet, *Cyclorrhynchus psittacula,* 10¼ in. Has the same distribution as the last species.
Crested Auklet, *Aethia cristatella,* 7 in. Found from the Arctic Ocean to the northern part of the Pacific.

(above) Beach Stone Curlew
(centre) Spotted Thicknee
(below) Stone Curlew

Crab Plovers

Crab Plover, *Dromas ardeola*, 13¼-16½ in.
The sole representative of the family
Dromadeidae. It inhabits the islands in
the northern part of the Indian Ocean,
as well as the coasts of north-east
Africa and the Persian Gulf. It goes
about in flocks, breeds in colonies and
lays its single egg in a long tunnel in
the sand.

Pratincoles

The pratincoles, Glareolidae, contain
about 17 species, found in the warmer
steppe and desert regions of Europe,
Africa, Asia and Australia.

Seebohm's Courser, *Rhinoptilus cinctus
seebohmi*, 9¾ in. Found in South Africa.
Cream-coloured Courser, *Cursorius cursor*, 9 in. Found in south-west Asia and
Africa; some may reach north Europe.
Egyptian Plover, *Pluvianus aegyptius*,
9 in. Found in Africa from Senegal to
Sudan. It buries its three eggs about 3 in.
down in the sand and the warmth of
the sun incubates them. In very hot
weather it lays itself down on the sand,

(from above) Seebohm's Courser; Cream-coloured Courser; Egyptian Plover; Pratincole

perhaps to protect the eggs against too
much heat. They were said to remove
pieces of food from the teeth of crocodiles.
Pratincole, *Glareola pratincola*, 9 in.
Breeds in parts of south Europe, and in
large areas of Africa and west Asia.

Sheathbills

The sheathbills, Chionididae, with only
two species, have a horny sheath cover-
ing the root of the bill.

Yellow-billed Sheathbill, *Chionis alba*,
16½ in. Breeds on South Georgia,
southern Orkneys and other sub-
antarctic islands.
Kerguelen Sheathbill, *Chionis minor*,
16½ in. Breeds on Kerguelen, Crozet and
Prince Edward Islands.

Crab Plover

Plovers

The plovers and waders, Charadriidae, form a large family of about 160 widely distributed species, living mainly in the cold temperate and Arctic regions. They feed almost exclusively on insects, larvae, worms and crustaceans.

Lapwing, *Vanellus vanellus*, 12 in. Breeds in north and central Europe and north Asia. It nests in cultivated land and in marsh areas, and is one of the commonest of all waders.
Grey-headed Lapwing, *Microsarcops cinereus*, 13½ in. Breeds in central Siberia, north China and Japan.
Red-wattled Lapwing, *Lobivanellus indicus*, 13 in. Found in southern Asia and common in cultivated areas.
Cayenne Lapwing, *Belonopterus cayennensis*, 12½ in. Found in South America.
Spur-winged Plover, *Lobibyx novaehollandiae*, 14 in. Found in Australia; it has spurs on the edges of the wings, as do some other plovers.

(from above) Lapwing; Grey-headed Lapwing; Red-wattled Lapwing

(above) Yellow-billed Sheathbill
(below) Kerguelen Sheathbill

Blacksmith Plover, *Hoplopterus armatus*, 11 in., from southern Africa, has spurs on the edges of the wings.
Sociable Plover, *Chettusia gregaria*, 11½ in. Found in the steppe regions of south Russia and south to Sudan and India.
Ringed Plover, *Charadrius hiaticula*, 7½ in. Breeds in north Europe and northernmost North America.
Little Ringed Plover, *Charadrius dubius*, 6 in. Breeds in Europe, except in the northernmost regions, as well as in north Africa and Asia.
Dotterel, *Charadrius morinellus*, 8½ in. Breeds on mountains and tundra in northernmost Europe and Asia, including north-east Scotland. The male normally incubates the eggs and looks after the young.

Grey Plover, *Charadrius squatarola,* 11 in. A high Arctic circumpolar breeding bird, which winters in the tropics.

Turnstone, *Arenaria interpres,* 9 in. Breeds along the coasts in Arctic and cold temperate regions. It hunts for insects under small stones which it moves away with the beak.

Kentish Plover, *Charadrius alexandrinus,* 6½ in. Found along the coasts of Europe (including south-east England), except in the northernmost regions, as well as in Africa, Asia and Australia.

Golden Plover, *Charadrius apricarius,* 11 in. Breeds in marshes and heathland in north Europe and north Asia.

Great Snipe, *Capella media,* 11 in. Breeds in Norway, north-east Europe and west Siberia.

Common Snipe, *Capella gallinago,* 10½ in. Breeds in north and central Europe and north Asia, and lives in meadows and marshes. During display flights a neighing sound is produced by air rushing

(from above) Cayenne Lapwing; Spur-winged Plover; Blacksmith Plover; Sociable Plover
(centre, from left) Ringed Plover; Little Ringed Plover; Dotterel; Grey Plover
(below) Turnstone; Kentish Plover; Golden Plover

through the widely spread outer tail-feathers.

Jack Snipe, *Lymnocryptes minimus,* 7½ in. Breeds in north Europe and in Siberia, usually in swampy areas.

Woodcock, *Scolopax rusticola,* 13½ in. Breeds in most of north and central Europe and in Asia north of the Himalayas. During its display flight the male flies low over the tree-tops.

Black-tailed Godwit, *Limosa limosa,* 16 in. Breeds in south-west Iceland, Belgium and eastwards to north Asia; many winter in the Mediterranean area.

Bar-tailed Godwit, *Limosa lapponica,* 15 in. Breeds in Arctic regions of Europe and Asia and winters in Britain and further south.

Curlew, *Numenius arquata,* 21-23 in. Breeds in north and central Europe and north Asia.

Whimbrel, *Numenius phaeopus,* 16 in. Breeds in northernmost Europe, Asia and north America.

Lesser Yellowlegs, *Tringa flavipes,* 10 in. Breeds in North America, and sometimes strays to Europe.

Green Sandpiper, *Tringa ochropus,* 9 in. Breeds in Scandinavia, east Europe and Siberia. A woodland bird that lays its eggs in old deserted nests in trees.

Dowitcher, *Limnodromus griseus,* 11½ in. Breeds in North America and sometimes strays to Europe.

Redshank, *Tringa totanus,* 11 in. Breeds in most parts of Europe and in Asia north of the Himalayas. It lives mostly in marsh or moorland areas.

Greenshank, *Tringa nebularia,* 12 in. Breeds in northernmost Europe and winters in the Mediterranean countries.

Wood Sandpiper, *Tringa glareola,* 8 in. Breeds in Scandinavia, east Europe and Siberia.

Buff-breasted Sandpiper, *Tryngites subruficollis,* 8 in. Breeds in North America and occasionally visits Europe.

(from above) Great Snipe; Common Snipe; Jack Snipe; Woodcock; Black-tailed Godwit; Bar-tailed Godwit; Curlew; Whimbrel

(above) Lesser Yellowlegs; Green Sandpiper; Dowitcher
(below) Redshank; Greenshank; Wood Sandpiper

Knot, *Calidris canutus,* 10 in. Breeds in the high Arctic and winters in west Europe and further south.

Sanderling, *Crocethia alba,* 8 in. A high Arctic circumpolar breeding bird that winters in South Africa, India, Australia and South America.

Ruff, *Philomachus pugnax,* 11½ in. Breeds in many parts of north Europe from north France and Norway eastwards;

it winters in Africa. An almost silent bird mostly found in coastal areas. The plumage of the males is very variable. The female, or reeve, makes the nest, incubates the eggs and rears the young.

Little Stint, *Calidris minuta,* 5¼ in. Breeds from Finmark in Norway to east Siberia and winters in south Africa and India.

Dunlin, *Calidris alpina,* 7 in. A common

(above) Buff-breasted Sandpiper; Knot; Sanderling
(below) Ruff; Little Stint; Dunlin; Common Sandpiper

breeding bird on coastal meadows in north Europe; it winters in west Europe and the Mediterranean.

Common Sandpiper, *Tringa hypoleucos,* 7¾ in. Breeds over almost the whole of Europe and north Asia and winters in South Africa.

Oystercatcher, *Haematopus ostralegus,* 17 in. Breeds along the coasts almost everywhere in the world, except in the polar regions. It feeds on sand-worms, crabs, snails and bivalves.

Black Oystercatcher, *Haemotopus o. unicolor,* 17 in. A form of the last species found in New Zealand. Similar forms occur elsewhere.

Avocet, *Recurvirostra avosetta,* 17 in. Breeds in relatively few parts of Europe, but in large areas of Africa and Asia. It skims the surface of the water with the bill for small crustaceans, worms, fish eggs and algae or moves it over the mud on the bottom. Unlike most waders it sometimes swims.

American Avocet, *Recurvirostra americana,* 17 in. Found in North America.

Black-winged Stilt, *Himantopus himantopus,* 15 in. Breeds in south France, Portugal, Spain, the Balkans, and large areas of Africa, Australia and America.

Black-necked Stilt, *Himantopus himantopus mexicanus,* 15 in. Found from the warmer regions of North America to Peru and Brazil.

Grey Phalarope, *Phalaropus fulicarius,* 8 in. An Arctic circumpolar breeding bird. In this species and in the red-necked phalarope it is the female that has the brighter plumage and the male that incubates the eggs and rears the young.

Wilson's Phalarope, *Steganopus tricolor,* 9 in. Breeds in North America and winters in South America.

Red-necked Phalarope, *Phalaropus lobatus,* 7 in. Breeds in the Arctic and in northernmost Europe.

(from above) Oystercatcher; Black Oystercatcher; Avocet; American Avocet; Black-winged Stilt; Black-necked Stilt; Grey Phalarope; Wilson's Phalarope; Red-necked Phalarope

Gulls

The gulls, Laridae, contain about 120 species, distributed over almost the whole of the globe. They are excellent fliers, but not particularly good swimmers. They feed on fish and other marine animals. Gulls usually go around in flocks and breed in colonies. The young hatch with a thick down and are beautifully patterned, but remain in or near the nest until they are fit to fly. The group contains the true gulls, terns and skuas as well as the less well known skimmers.

Black-headed Gull, *Larus ridibundus,* 15 in. Widespread and abundant in north and central Europe from Iceland, Britain and east France eastwards into Asia to Kamtchatka. It feeds principally on insects, worms, snails, bivalves and offal and to a limited extent on small fish. It winters in west and south

(above, from left) Black-headed Gull; Ivory Gull; Glaucous Gull; Iceland Gull *(then, from above)* Little Gull; Franklin's Gull; Heermann's Gull; Sabine's Gull; Common Gull; Herring Gull; Great Black-backed Gull

Europe. In winter the sooty-brown skull cap is reduced to a single spot behind the eye.

Ivory Gull, *Pagophila eburnea,* 17½ in. Breeds in colonies in the high Arctic, and feeds on carrion and seal droppings.

Glaucous Gull, *Larus hyperboreus,* 26-32 in. Breeds in the Arctic, amongst other places in Greenland, Iceland and on the coasts of the Bering Sea.

Iceland Gull, *Larus glaucoides,* 22-26 in. Breeds in Greenland and Iceland.

Little Gull, *Larus minutus,* 11 in. Breeds in Denmark and further eastwards in north Europe and north Asia.

Franklin's Gull, *Larus pipixcan,* 13½ in. Breeds on the coasts of North America and in large colonies on the prairies.

Heermann's Gull, *Larus heermanni,* 17 in. Breeds on the west coast of North America.

Sabine's Gull, *Xema sabini,* 13 in. Breeds in the high Arctic. The only gull which has a truly cleft tail.

Common Gull, *Larus canus,* 16 in. Breeds in north Europe, including parts of Britain, and in Siberia and north-west North America. It feeds on fish offal, carrion, insects, eggs and young of birds, and breeds in colonies.

Herring Gull, *Larus argentatus,* 22 in. Breeds in the Arctic regions and along nearly all the coasts of Europe. It feeds on shore animals, fish offal and the eggs and young of birds.

Great Black-backed Gull, *Larus marinus,* 29 in. Breeds along the coasts of north Europe, Iceland, Greenland, and

(from above) Common Tern; Arctic Tern; Roseate Tern;
Sandwich Tern; Gull-billed Tern; Caspian Tern; Little Tern

(*above*) Black Tern; Whiskered Tern; (*centre*) Royal Tern; Inca Tern
(*below*) White-winged Black Tern; Sooty Tern

elsewhere in the Arctic. It feeds on fish, the eggs and young of birds, rats and rabbits as well as berries, seaweed and algae.

Common Tern, *Sterna hirundo,* 14 in. Found nearly everywhere in Europe, west Asia, north Africa and in the eastern part of north America. The north European terns fly to west Europe in August and return at the end of April.

Arctic Tern, *Sterna paradisaea,* 15½ in. Breeds in Europe, Asia, the Arctic, North America and winters in the Antarctic. It closely resembles the common tern but its red beak lacks a black point.

Roseate Tern, *Sterna dougalli,* 15 in. Breeds along the coasts of the Atlantic from Nova Scotia to the West Indies and locally in Britain and France.

Sandwich Tern, *Thalasseus sandvicensis,* 16 in. Breeds in crowded colonies along the coasts of Britain, Holland, Denmark, South Sweden and some parts of the Mediterranean.

Gull-billed Tern, *Gelochelidon nilotica,* 15 in. Breeds in Denmark, Holland, south Spain, south France, Bulgaria, west Asia and north Africa. It nests in colonies on sandy beaches and feeds amongst other things on beetles and lizards.

White Tern

Caspian Tern, *Hydroprogne caspia,* 21 in. Breeds locally in Europe and in Africa, Asia, Australia and north America. It feeds almost exclusively on small fish, which it dives for from a height.
Little Tern, *Sterna albifrons,* 9½ in. A common breeding bird along most of the European coastline.
Black Tern, *Chlidonias niger,* 9½ in. Breeds in inland waters in Denmark, central Europe, south Spain and west Asia, and feeds mainly on insects and small aquatic animals.
Whiskered Tern, *Chlidonias hybrida,* 9¾ in. Breeds in Portugal, Spain, south-west France and parts of east Europe; other forms are found in south Asia, Australia and Africa.
Royal Tern, *Thalasseus maximus,* 19 in. Lives along the coasts of north and central America.
Inca Tern, *Larosterna inca,* 15½ in. Found along the west coast of South America, and easily distinguished by the white curly moustache of feathers running over the cheek from the bill to the neck.
White-winged Black Tern, *Chlidonias leucopterus,* 9¼ in. Breeds in east Europe and west and central Asia.
Sooty Tern, *Sterna fuscata,* 16 in. Breeds (as different races) on tropical and sub-tropical islands in the Atlantic, Pacific and Indian Oceans.
White Tern, *Gygis alba,* 12½ in. Breeds on several island groups in tropical and subtropical seas. It nests in colonies and lays its single egg on a cliff ledge, on a horizontal branch or on a palm leaf.
Long-tailed Skua, *Stercorarius longicaudus,* 21 in. Breeds in the high Arctic and southwards to Scandinavia.
Arctic Skua, *Stercorarius parasiticus,* 18 in. Breeds in the high Arctic and southwards to Nova Scotia, Scandinavia and north Scotland. Like other skuas it gets most of its food by chasing gulls and making them disgorge their prey which it then catches in the air.

(above) Long-tailed Skua; Arctic Skua; *(below)* Great Skua; Pomatorhine Skua

Great Skua, *Stercorarius skua,* 23 in. Breeds in the Arctic regions, Iceland, Faeroes, Orkney and Shetlands. In winter it migrates southwards over the Atlantic.

Pomatorhine Skua, *Stercorarius pomarinus,* 20 in. Breeds on the Arctic coasts of Asia, north America and Greenland.

Black Skimmer, *Rhynchops nigra,* 15-19 in. Found along the Atlantic coast of America from New Brunswick to Argentina and along the Pacific coast from Ecuador to Chile; they nest in large colonies. They feed mainly at twilight flying over the surface with open bill so that the long lower mandible ploughs through the water. In this way they catch insects and small fish from the surface.

Indian Skimmer, *Rhynchops albicollis,* 15½ in. Found in south Asia.

(from above) Little Bustard; Houbara Bustard; Great Bustard

(above) Black Skimmer
(below) Indian Skimmer

Cranes

IN ADDITION TO THE TRUE CRANES the order Gruiformes contains the bustards, cariamas, sun-bitterns, kagus, mesites, sun-grebes and the rails and coots. In this book the last three groups come immediately after the seed-snipe and jacanas which are now classified with the gulls and waders, Charadriiformes.

Bustards

The bustards are medium-sized to large birds which can run fast but seldom fly. They live on open land, mostly in Africa, a few in Europe and Asia and a single one in Australia.

(above) Kori Bustard
(below) Heuglin's Bustard

Little Bustard, *Tetrax tetrax,* 17 in. Breeds in north-west Africa, south Europe and west Asia; it is only the size of a domestic fowl.

Houbara Bustard, *Chlamydotis undulata,* 25 in. Found in the Canary Islands, in the Sahara and in the desert regions of west Asia. Both sexes have a collar of large feathers on the sides of the neck.

Great Bustard, *Otis tarda,* male 40 in., female 30 in. The male is the world's heaviest flying bird and Europe's largest bird. The differences in weight between the sexes is the largest in any bird species, as the male weighs 24-35 lb., the female only 11-13 lb. The great bustard breeds in Spain, east Germany, Poland, Rumania and south Russia as well as in north Africa and large parts of Asia. When danger threatens, it flees by running and will only take to the air if surprised. It feeds mostly on plant food, such as kale, clover and roots, but also takes many insects, worms, frogs, lizards and small rodents. During courtship the male brings the tail feathers up over the back, lays his head backwards and puffs out the throat pouch so that the beard bristles stand erect.

Kori Bustard, *Choriotis kori,* 44-52 in. Found in open country in East and South Africa.

Heuglin's Bustard, *Neotis heuglini,* 35 in. Found in north-east Africa.

Cranes

The true cranes, limpkins and trumpeters, Grues, are a small group of widely distributed birds.

(above, from left) Crane; Lilford's Crane
(below) Demoiselle Crane

The 14 species of *true cranes* are found nearly everywhere in temperate and tropical regions, except in South America. The wings are large and broad, and the inner secondary feathers are elongated to form ornamental plumes. The neck and wind-pipe are very long.

Crane, *Grus grus*, 45 in. Breeds in east Scandinavia, Denmark, north Germany

(above) Sandhill Crane; Whooping Crane; Sarus Crane; Australian Crane
(centre) Manchurian Crane; Hooded Crane; Stanley Crane; Wattled Crane; West African Crowned Crane; *(below)* Black-necked Crane; White-naped Crane

and further east into Siberia; also in Yugoslavia. It is a typical migratory bird and winters in southern Europe, north Africa and India. It usually flies in flocks of 20 to 40 individuals arranged in wedges or wavy lines. In the courtship both sexes extend the wings, stretch the neck forwards and jump up and down, whilst trumpeting. They nest in marshes and bogs and lay two eggs, as do the other cranes. The young are able to leave the nest shortly after the eggs have hatched, but are not able to fly for about four months.

Lilford's Crane, *Grus grus lilfordi*, 44 in. A form of the common crane found in central and east Asia.

Demoiselle Crane, *Anthropoides virgo*, 38 in. Breeds in south-east Europe, south Russia, large parts of Asia as well as in north Africa. It lives on steppe land and spends the winter in south Asia and north Africa.

Sandhill Crane, *Grus canadensis*, 35-47 in. Breeds in north-east Siberia and Arctic Canada, and also to the south.

Whooping Crane, *Grus americana*, 48 in. Formerly common on the prairies of North America, but now very reduced in numbers. The wind-pipe is longer than that of any other bird.

Sarus Crane, *Grus antigone*, 70 in. Found from south Asia to Australia, and common in rice plantations and on small lakes. It feeds mostly on mice, snakes and insects, and the pairs mate for life, as do other cranes.

Australian Crane, *Grus rubicunda*, 40 in. Found both in New Guinea and in Australia.

Manchurian Crane, *Grus japonensis*, 50 in. Breeds in Manchuria and Korea, and winters in China.

Hooded Crane, *Grus monacha*, 35 in. Found in north-east Asia.

Stanley Crane, *Anthropoides paradisea*, 41 in. Found in the high veld of South Africa south of the Zambesi. The breast- and some wing-feathers are very long.

Great African Wattled Crane, *Bugeranus carunculatus*, 46 in. Found in east and south Africa.

West African Crowned Crane, *Balerica pavonina*, 41 in. Found in Africa and is widely distributed on the savannas of west Africa. Unlike other cranes it sometimes perches in trees.

Black-necked Crane, *Grus nigricollis*, 42 in. Breeds in central Asia.

White-naped Crane, *Grus vipio*, 42 in. Breeds in central Asia.

Southern Limpkin, *Aramus scolopaceus*, 26 in. Found in south America.

Limpkin, *Aramus guarauna*, 26½ in. Found from Florida to Argentina. It

(from above) Southern Limpkin; Limpkin

Cariamas

The cariamas, Cariamae, contain only two species, with short bills, long necks and very long legs with short toes. They are essentially steppe birds which go about in pairs or in small flocks; they run fast but seldom fly.

Burmeister's Cariama, *Chunga burmeisteri*, 29 in. Found in north-west Argentina. It usually nests in trees or bushes.

Crested Cariama, *Cariama cristata*, 33 in. Found on the tableland of Brazil, Paraguay and north Argentina. It feeds mostly on grasshoppers and other insects but also takes lizards, snakes and small animals.

(above) White-winged Trumpeter; Green-winged Trumpeter; *(below)* Ochre-winged Trumpeter

lives in marshes and bogs, where it hunts with its beak for snails and bivalves. It builds a large nest in bushes or trees.

White-winged Trumpeter, *Psophia leucoptera leucoptera*, 21 in. Found principally in Peru and north Brazil. The trumpeters go about in flocks on the floor of the forest and feed largely on fruits, seeds, snails and larvae. They run fast but fly seldom and badly. They have a characteristic and noisy dance.

Green-winged Trumpeter, *Psophia viridis*, 21 in. Found principally in Brazil.

Ochre-winged Trumpeter, *Psophia leucoptera ochroptera*, 19 in. Found in north-west Brazil.

(above) Burmeister's Cariama
(below) Crested Cariama

Sun-bittern

Kagu

Sun-bitterns

Sun-bittern, *Eurypyga helias,* 19½ in. Lives along forest-clad rivers and marshes in America from Guatemala to tropical South America. It prefers sunshine but is also found often in shady places along the rivers. The food consists of insects, small fish, frogs and lizards, which it seizes with its pointed bill. It moves about slowly, with rather precise steps, and usually keeps the body horizontal. When excited it has a form of display in which the broad wings and tail are spread to show the brilliant markings.

Kagus

Kagu, *Rhinochetos jubatus,* 22 in. Found only on New Caledonia in the Pacific, and now almost extinct. The long feather crest on the top of the head can be erected. The wing feathers are soft and flight is poor. It lives in the mountains and is mainly nocturnal; by day it sleeps in crevices in the cliffs. The food consists of worms and snails. When displaying the wings are spread to reveal a series of black, white and rust-coloured spots.

Seed-snipe

THE SEED-SNIPE, Thinocoridae, are a group of 4 species all found in South America, and often classified among the waders, Charadriiformes (p. 158). They have a short bill, long pointed wings and short legs and feet. Some live in mountain regions above the tree belt and feed on seeds and buds.

Gay's Seed-snipe, *Attagis gayi,* 11½ in. Found in the Andes of Peru and Chile del Fuego, at heights up to 15,000 ft.

Gay's Seed-snipe

(above) Pheasant-tailed Jacana
(below) White-necked Jacana; African Jacana; Bronze-winged Jacana

Jacanas

THE JACANAS are long-necked tropical marsh birds with long pointed wings which bear a horny spur and very lengthened toes and claws. They walk about on floating plants. The jacanas are now usually classified close to the waders (Charadriiformes, p. 158).

(left) South American Jacana
(right) another race of the same

White-necked Jacana, *Actophilornis albinucha,* 11 in. Found only in Madagascar.

African Jacana, *Actophilornis africanus,* 11 in. Widely distributed in Africa south of the Sahara.

Pheasant-tailed Jacana, *Hydrophasianus chirurgus,* 19½ in. Found in India and Indonesia. It has a small spur on the shank and a very sharp wing spur.

Bronze-winged Jacana, *Metopidius indicus,* 11 in. Found in India and in Indonesia.

South American Jacana, *Jacana spinosa jacana,* 9½ in. Found in Trinidad and north-eastern South America. Often known as the spur-wing, from the long pointed spur on the edge of the wing. It occurs in two phases, one completely black, the other red-brown, often in the same population.

Jacana spinosa spinosa, (also illustrated), is another race found in many parts of central America.

Unicoloured Mesites

parts of the world. They live either alone or in pairs along thickly wooded tropical and subtropical rivers. The food consists of seeds, aquatic insects, crustaceans, snails and small frogs, but otherwise very little is known about their habits.

Masked Finfoot, *Heliopais personata,* 22 in. Found in Bengal, south-east Asia and Sumatra. A rare bird that dives and swims well.

African Finfoot, *Podica senegalensis,* 16 in. Widespread in Africa south of the Sahara.

Sun-grebe, *Heliornis fulica,* 12 in. Found from Mexico southwards to north Argentina; it keeps mostly to vegetation along the rivers.

Mesites

THE MESITES, Mesoenatidae, are a small group of birds confined to Madagascar. They live in the forests and run fast but seldom fly, although the wings are well developed.

Unicoloured Mesites, *Mesoenas unicolor,* 7 in. A rare bird that lives on the floors of damp rain forests.

Sun-grebes

THE SUN-GREBES, Heliornithes, have a superficial resemblance to the grebes; the neck is long, the wings long and pointed, and the feet are short with a web round the front toes as in the coots. The plumage is compact and close. The three species in the group are all very similar although they live in different

(from above) Masked Finfoot; African Finfoot; Sun-grebe

Crested Coot; American Coot; Coot

Rails and Coots

THE RAILS AND COOTS, Rallidae, form a large group of birds within the order Gruiformes; they are found nearly everywhere except in the Arctic and Antarctic. The body is more laterally compressed than in other birds, and this is probably correlated with their ability to penetrate thick vegetation. Most of them have a small claw on the end of the first digit of the wing.

Crested Coot, *Fulica cristata*, 16 in. Breeds in Africa and south Spain, occasionally straying to France and Italy.

American Coot, *Fulica americana*, 15 in. Widespread in North America and the West Indies.

Coot, *Fulica atra*, 15 in. Breeds throughout Europe, except in the northernmost regions, as well as in Asia, New Guinea and Australia. It lives in the reed belt along large and small lakes, and feeds both on plant food and small animals; in shallow water it dives for water plants, which it brings to the surface and picks clean of snails and other small aquatic animals. Many coots migrate and are seen in large flocks during winter.

White-breasted Waterhen, *Amaurornis phoenicurus*, 12 in. Widespread in south Asia, and often seen in marshes and paddy fields.

Moorhen, *Gallinula chloropus*, 13 in. Found everywhere in Europe, except in the northernmost regions, and in many other parts of the world. It keeps mostly

(above) White-breasted Waterhen;
(centre) Moorhen; *(below)* Weka

to the water, but often spends the night in trees and bushes. The food consists of worms, snails, insects, berries, seeds and water plants.

Weka, *Gallirallus australis,* 19 in. Found in New Zealand, where it feeds on lizards, mice, rats and eggs.

Clapper Rail, *Rallus longirostris,* 15 in. Widely distributed in America, mainly on the coasts.

Water Rail, *Rallus aquaticus,* 11 in. Breeds throughout Europe, except in north Scandinavia, as well as in north Africa and north Asia. A difficult bird to observe, as it lives sheltered on lakes and marshes and moves about mostly at night in the luxuriant vegetation on the edges of lakes, feeding on insects, larvae, worms, snails, seeds and berries.

Sora, *Porzana carolina,* 7½ in. Breeds in North America and winters to the south.

Spotted Crake, *Porzana porzana,* 9 in. Breeds throughout most of Europe and west Asia, nesting along the edges of ponds, marshes, lakes and rivers. It feeds on insects, snails and other small aquatic animals, as well as seeds of water plants.

Baillon's Crake, *Porzana pusilla,* 7 in. Breeds in Portugal, Spain, France, north Italy, north Balkans, north Africa and west Asia.

King Rail, *Rallus elegans,* 14 in. Breeds in large areas of the interior of North America southwards to north Mexico and south Florida.

Platen's Rail, *Aramidopsis plateni,* 12 in. Found only on Celebes.

Black Rail, *Laterallus jamaicensis,* 5 in. Widespread in temperate North America.

Corncrake, *Crex crex,* 10½ in. Found as a breeding bird in central Europe and further northwards to Scotland, south

(from above) Clapper Rail; Water Rail; Sora; Spotted Crake; Baillon's Crake; King Rail; Platen's Rail; Black Rail

(from above) Corncrake; <u>Watercock;</u> Naked-
headed Rail; Allen's Gallinule; Purple Gallinule;
Grey-headed Gallinule; American Purple
Gallinule; Takahe

Norway and south Finland, as well as
in large parts of west Asia. It migrates
and winters in southern Europe, Africa
and India. It is very shy and wary and
lives mostly sheltered in high grass. The
food consists of insects, worms, snails
and seeds. The nest is found sheltered in
clover and grass fields, marshes and meadows and consists of a scraped hollow
with a little dry grass lining.

Watercock, *Gallicrex cinerea,* 17 in.
Found in India and south-east Asia and
common in Bengal and Assam.

Naked-headed Rail, *Gymnocrex rosen-
bergi,* 12 in. Found only in Celebes.

Allen's Gallinule, *Porphyrula alleni,*
10 in. Widespread in Africa south of the
Sahara.

Purple Gallinule, *Porphyrio porphyrio,*
19 in. Breeds in south Spain, Sardinia,
Sicily and north Africa, and occasionally
strays northwards to France and central
Europe. It has a peculiar hooting cry.

Grey-headed Gallinule, *Porphyrio poliocephalus,* 16½ in. Found in south Asia
and the Indo-Australian Islands.

American Purple Gallinule, *Porphyrula martinicia,* 13 in. Breeds from southern United States to central South
America. It feeds on seeds and aquatic
insects, and may sometimes do damage
in rice, maize and banana plantations.
It also takes the eggs and young of
birds and may become truly predatory,
attacking for example ducklings which
it kills with a blow on the back of the
head.

Takahe, *Notornis hochstetteri,* 19½ in. A
flightless New Zealand land bird about
the size of a small goose. It was first
observed in 1849, thought to have died
out around 1900, but was re-discovered
in 1949. There are now 30-35 individuals
in the uplands of South Island.

(from above) Pallas's Sandgrouse; Pin-tailed Sandgrouse; Black-bellied Sandgrouse

Pallas's Sandgrouse, *Syrrhaptes paradoxus,* 14-16 in. Found on the steppes of Asia from Kazakstan to Mongolia and west China. At irregular intervals they undertake mass migrations and spread themselves over almost the whole of Europe. The largest European invasions took place in 1863 and 1888 and the last one in 1908. In 1888 they managed to breed in several places, amongst others in Britain and west Jutland. A few years after such an invasion they have all disappeared.

Pintailed Sandgrouse, *Pterocles alchata,* 12½ in. Breeds in south France, Portugal, Spain, north Africa, south Russia and south-west Asia.

Black-bellied Sandgrouse, *Pterocles orientalis,* 14 in. Breeds in Portugal, Spain, north Africa and south-west Asia.

Double-banded Sandgrouse, *Pterocles bicinctus,* 10¼ in. Found on the savannas of south Africa.

Pigeons

THE ORDER COLUMBIFORMES contains the sandgrouse and the true pigeons and doves.

The sandgrouse, Pteroclididae, are a small group which resemble true grouse more than the pigeons. They have long pointed wings and the very short legs are feather-clad to the toes; the three front toes are partly united. Sandgrouse are very fast and tenacious fliers. They live in large flocks on steppes and deserts mostly in Africa but also in south Asia, as well as in two places in south Europe. They feed almost exclusively on seeds. When they drink the beak is held under the water as in the pigeons.

(above) Double-banded Sandgrouse
(below) Yellow-throated Sandgrouse

(left, from above) White-crowned Pigeon; Turtle Dove; <u>Collared Turtle Dove;</u> Peaceful Dove
(right, from above) Wood Pigeon; Rock Dove; Stock Dove

Yellow-throated Sandgrouse, *Pterocles gutturalis,* 12½ in. Found along the rivers of south Africa.

Pigeons

The pigeons, Columbidae, are found almost everywhere, except in the Arctic and Antarctic, but mostly in tropical America and the Indo-Australian region. They feed on seeds and fruits. The young are fed with pigeon milk, a thick semi-liquid, which is formed in the crop of the parents. The extinct dodos of Mauritius were in a closely related family.

White-crowned Pigeon, *Columba leucocephala,* 13¼ in. Breeds in Florida and in some islands in the West Indies.

Turtle Dove, *Streptopelia turtur,* 11 in. Breeds in central and south Europe (including England), north Africa and west Asia and winters mainly in Africa.

Collared Turtle Dove, *Streptopelia deca-octo,* 11 in. Found over most of south Asia and in the last 20 years has spread through Turkey to the Balkans, Hungary, Austria, Germany, Denmark, south Sweden and Britain.

Peaceful Dove, *Geopelia striata placida,* 9 in. Found in Australia.

Wood Pigeon, *Columba palumbus,* 16 in. Breeds throughout Europe, except ·in the northernmost regions, in north-west Africa and west Asia; it is Europe's largest pigeon. It feeds on mast, corn and many other foods. The flat nest is built of twigs and branches, which are so loosely put together that one can often see the two white eggs from below. Newly laid eggs can be found from the end of March to the end of September, so it probably breeds 3 to 4 times in the year. Before the first clutch of young can look after themselves, the parents build a new nest and manage to feed the older young and incubate the new eggs.

Stock Dove, *Columba oenas,* 13 in. Breeds in most parts of Europe, except in the northernmost regions, and in north-west Africa and west Asia. It nests in hollow trees and lays its eggs on the existing tree mould. It most often lays two clutches. Stock doves are migratory birds and usually winter in west and south Europe.

Rock Dove, *Columba livia,* 13 in. Breeds in the Faeroes, Orkneys, Ireland, Scotland, south Europe, north Africa and west Asia. It lives on rocky coasts and nests in cliff crevices and caves. This is the original form of the tame pigeon.

Namaqua Dove, *Oena capensis,* 10 in. Widespread in Africa south of the Sahara, and in Arabia and Madagascar.

Tooth-billed Pigeon, *Didunculus strigi-rostris,* 11½ in. Found only on two islands of Samoa. It goes about in the tree-tops, but sometimes comes down to the ground. The food consists of fruits, particularly figs. The edge of the lower mandible is notched.

Nicobar Pigeon, *Caloenas nicobarica,* 14 in. Widespread from the Nicobar Islands in the west through the Indo-Australian Archipelago to the Solomon Islands, but only on the small islands.

(above) Namaqua Dove; Tooth-billed Pigeon; Nicobar Pigeon
(below) Common Crowned Pigeon; Victoria Crowned Pigeon; Bleeding-heart Pigeon

(above) Green Pigeon; Many-coloured Fruit Dove; Seychelle Pigeon; Nutmeg Pigeon
(below) Charming Fruit Dove; Pheasant Pigeon

Common Crowned Pigeon, *Goura cristata,* 29 in. Found in western New Guinea. It lives in small flocks in marshes and woodland where it searches for fallen fruit and spends the night on low branches.

Victoria Crowned Pigeon, *Goura victoria,* 31 in. Found in New Guinea, and is the largest of all the pigeons.

Bleeding-heart Pigeon, *Callicolumba luzonica,* 10 in. Found in the rain forests of the Philippines where it goes about on the forest floor. Named from the blood-red spot on the white breast.

Green Pigeon, *Treron calva,* 11 in. Widespread in Africa south of the Sudan, except in the most southerly regions; there are several races.

Many-coloured Fruit Dove, *Ptilinopus perusii,* 8¼ in. Found in Samoa, Sunda, Fiji and Tonga. It seldom moves except when searching for fruit which it swallows whole.

Seychelle Pigeon, *Alectroenas pulcherrima,* 10 in. Found on the Seychelles. It has warty growths at the root of the bill.

Nutmeg Pigeon, *Ducula spilorrhoa,* 15½ in. Found from New Guinea to north and east Australia. It lives in the trees and seldom comes to the ground. Many of these pigeons feed on nutmegs.

Charming Fruit Dove, *Ptilinopus bellus,* 15½ in. Found in New Guinea.

Pheasant Pigeon, *Otidiphaps nobilis cervicalis,* 17½ in. Found in the mountains of eastern New Guinea.

Hemipodes

THE BUSTARD-QUAILS and collared hemipodes, Turnices, are a small group usually now classified among the Gruiformes. They are found in the tropics and subtropics of south Europe, Africa, Asia and Australia, where they live in open country. They are small seed-eating birds, which superficially resemble the quails. The female is larger and more mottled than the male and lives in polyandry. The males take care of incubation and rear the young.

Hottentot Button-quail, *Turnix hottentotta,* 6 in. Found in the southern part of Cape Province, South Africa.

Yellow-legged Button-quail, *Turnix tanki,* 5½ in. Found in India, south-east Asia, China, the Andaman and Nicobar Islands.

Red-backed Button-quail, *Turnix maculosa,* 6 in. Found in New Guinea and Australia.

Andalusian Hemipode, *Turnix sylvatica,* 6 in. Found in large areas of Africa and of Asia south of the Himalayas; in addition it also breeds in south Portugal and south Spain. It lives on grassy steppes and savannas, and very seldom flies.

Quail-plover, *Ortyxelos meiffrenii,* 4½ in. Found on dry grassy plains in Africa. The male and the female are nearly the same size.

Collared Hemipode, *Pedionomus torquatus,* 4-5 in. Widespread in the dry regions of Australia, where it is known as the Plain Wanderer. It feeds on seeds and insects in grassy areas and is the only representative of its family.

(from above) Hottentot Button-quail; Yellow-legged Button-quail; Red-backed Button-quail; Andalusian Hemipode; Quail-plover; Collared Hemipode

Hoatzin

second digits on the wing, each of which has a powerful claw used for climbing trees. The wing claws are reduced to small horny knobs in the adults.

Fowls

The fowls and their relatives in the sub-order Galli all have one of the four toes directed backwards, and the male usually has a spur on the shank. The crop is very roomy and the gizzard thick-walled. The fowls are found nearly everywhere except in the Antarctic. They are vegetarian land birds and do not fly particularly well. Many are polygamous, and the female only incubates the eggs. The group may be divided into three families: the curassows, the brush turkeys and the pheasants.

Curassows

The curassows, Cracidae, are found from Arizona and Mexico and further southwards to southern South America. The majority feed on fruits in the tree-tops of the rain forests; but the largest species find other food on the ground and eat many small animals.

Fowls

THE ORDER GALLIFORMES includes fowls, pheasants, partridges, turkeys and quails in the large sub-order Galli, and the hoatzin as the sole representative of the sub-order Opisthocomi.

Hoatzin, *Opisthocomus hoatzin,* 23 in. Found in northern South America east of the Andes, especially in marshy woodland and in trees along the edges of rivers. It goes about mostly in twilight and on moonlit nights, and flies heavily and slowly. The large muscular crop can deal with the thick leaves on which the hoatzin feeds, and has thus taken over the role of the gizzard, which is much reduced. The nest is always built in trees which stretch out over the water and it lays two to three eggs. The almost naked young can freely move the first and

Great Curassow, *Crax rubra,* 30-38 in. Found in the forests from Mexico through central America to Ecuador. The female is significantly smaller than the male and has no knob at the root of the bill.

Yarrell's Curassow, *Crax carunculata,* 35 in. Found in south-east Brazil.

Crested Curassow, *Crax nigra,* 37 in. Found in the northern part of South America, particularly in the Amazon region.

Galeated Curassow, *Pauxi pauxi,* 31 in.

(from left) Great Curassow; Yarrell's Curassow; Crested Curassow

Widespread in South America from Venezuela to Peru.

Razor-billed Curassow, *Mitu mitu,* 33 in. Found in South America.

White-eyebrowed Guan, *Penelope superciliaris,* 25 in. Found in flocks in the forests along the east coast of Brazil, living almost exclusively in the trees.

Piping Guan, *Pipile cumanensis,* 25 in. Found in South America.

Brush Turkeys

The brush turkeys, Megapodidae, are a small family found in Australia, New Guinea and neighbouring islands; they feed on juicy roots, seeds, fallen fruits, worms, snails and insects. The eggs make up 15% of the bird's weight (a hen's egg only 4%) and have a very large yolk. The incubation period is three times as long as that of a domestic hen's egg.

(above) Galeated Curassow; Razor-billed Curassow
(below) White-eyebrowed Guan; Piping Guan

(*above*) Incubator Bird; Great-headed Maleo
(*centre*) Pelew Brush Turkey; (*below*) Mallee Fowl; Brush Turkey

Brush turkeys leave the job of incubation to the warmth of the sun, volcanic ash or rotting vegetation. They make a mound of earth, leaves and twigs, often 6-9 ft. high and 18 ft. wide. At the top of this the female digs a series of three-foot holes, one for each of the 5-8 eggs. The newly hatched young work themselves out of the mound and seek shelter in the undergrowth; the plumage is well developed and the young can literally fly or flutter out from the nest mound.

Incubator Bird, *Megapodius cumingi,* 13 in. Found on the Philippines.

Great-headed Maleo, *Macrocephalon maleo,* 21 in. Found in the mountain forests of Celebes. The birds go down to the coast and bury their eggs in the black lava sand.

Pelew Brush Turkey, *Megapodius senex,* 12 in. Found on the Pelew Islands in the Pacific.

Mallee Fowl, *Leipoa ocellata,* 25 in. Found in southern Australia. It mostly uses decaying vegetation for the egg mound.

Brush Turkey, *Alectura lathami,* 25 in. Found in eastern Australia. The nest mound is sometimes 9 ft. high.

Pheasants

The pheasants, Phasianidae, are a large group found over the whole of the globe except in the coldest regions. The group contains the guineafowl, turkeys, grouse, true pheasants and American quails.

Many *guineafowls* have a naked head and neck, and the spurs are very short or lacking. They are all found in Africa but one of them extends to Arabia.

Black Guineafowl, *Phasidus niger,* 17 in. A rare bird of the forests of west Africa.

White-breasted Guineafowl, *Agelastes meleagrides,* 17 in. Found in the forests of tropical west Africa, but very rare.

Kenya Crested Guineafowl, *Guttera pucherani,* 19 in. Found in the coastal regions of east Africa.

Zambesi Crested Guineafowl, *Guttera edouardi,* 19 in. Found in south and east Africa.

Damaraland Helmet Guineafowl, *Numida meleagris damarensis,* 22 in. A race of the next species found in south-west Africa.

Helmet Guineafowl, *Numida meleagris,* 22 in. Found in numerous races over nearly the whole of Africa and in south-west Arabia. It feeds on seeds, berries and leaves as well as grasshoppers and other insects. The eggs are relatively thick-shelled.

Vulturine Guineafowl, *Acryllium vulturinum,* 28 in. Found in the tropical regions of East Africa.

The *turkeys,* with only two species found in north and central America, have naked warty skin on the head and neck and a flap of skin hangs down from the forehead. The male has a tassel of feathers on the breast.

(left, from above) Black Guineafowl; White-breasted Guineafowl
(centre, from above) Kenya Crested Guineafowl; Zambesi Crested Guineafowl;
Damaraland Helmet Guineafowl
(right, from above) Helmet Guineafowl; Vulturine Guineafowl

(from left) Turkey, male and female; Ocellated Turkey

Turkey, *Meleagris gallopavo*, 39-42 in. Found in southern United States and Mexico, mainly in oak and pine forests in the mountains. It feeds on fruits, berries, buds and grass as well as grasshoppers, frogs and lizards. The male usually collects 2 to 3 females; but after mating he pays no attention either to them or to the young. The turkey was introduced into Europe over 400 years ago and is now domesticated in many different countries.

Ocellated Turkey, *Agriocharis ocellata*, 35 in. Found in Yucatan and neighbouring parts of Guatemala and British Honduras, living in scrub forests and open country.

The *grouse* are distributed over large parts of the northern hemisphere, particularly in the conifer forest region. Unlike other birds many of them shed the horny sheath on the bill and claws after the breeding season. Grouse are all non-migratory.

Spruce Grouse, *Canachites canadensis*, 15-17 in. Found in the conifer forests of Canada and northern United States. The male displays on a fallen tree or on low branches.

Hazel Hen, *Tetrastes bonasia*, 14 in. Breeds in large areas of north and central Europe from east France eastward to Siberia. It lives mostly in mixed forest with thick undergrowth and feeds on berries, buds and small leaves. The male carries out his courtship dance alone, usually in a sheltered place.

Black Grouse, *Lyrurus tetrix*, male 21 in., female 16 in. Breeds in Britain and from east France eastwards into central Europe, also in north Europe and north Asia. The cleft tail of the large males is lyre-shaped; the smaller female is rust-brown with dark cross markings. They live in birch and conifer woods and on heaths, and feed on buds, leaves and berries. In spring the males come together in open places, known as leks, for their courtship display.

Blue Grouse, *Dendragapus obscurus,* 18-20 in. Found in western North America, where there are several races. The nest is on the ground, but the bird seeks shelter among trees.

Capercaillie, *Tetrao urogallus,* male 34 in., female 24 in. Breeds in the Pyrenees, Scotland, large parts of central Europe, Norway, Sweden, Finland, Russia and further east into Asia. The female is rust-brown with dark cross markings and is significantly smaller than the male. They feed on conifer shoots and buds and on berries and insect larvae. The courtship dance of the male takes place on the ground or on a low branch; the chin beard is stuck out and the rounded tail is held erect like a fan, whilst he produces a drumming sound. Capercaillies are polygamous, and after mating the males pay no attention to either the females or the young.

Greater Prairie Chicken, *Tympanuchus cupido,* 18 in. Found in west Canada and southern U.S.A. During display the males inflate the orange air sacs on the sides of the neck.

(above) Spruce Grouse; Hazel Hen; Black Grouse; *(below)* Blue Grouse; Capercaillie

Sage Grouse, *Centrocercus urophasianus,* 22-27 in. Found in western U.S.A. During the courtship display the male holds his tail erect like a fan and inflates the air sacs on the side of the neck so that they resemble oranges.

Red Grouse, *Lagopus scoticus,* 15 in. Breeds in Scotland, north England and Ireland, where it lives on heaths and moors. Unlike the willow grouse and ptarmigan it does not assume a winter plumage. The feet are feather-clad to the tips.

Willow Grouse, *Lagopus lagopus,* 16 in. Breeds in Norway, north Sweden, Finland and Russia as well as in north Asia

and northern North America. It has both a red-brown summer and autumn plumage and a completely white winter plumage. It lives mostly in birch and willow scrub and feeds on buds, crowberries and blueberries.

Ptarmigan, *Lagopus mutus,* 14 in. Breeds in the Pyrenees, the Alps and in the mountains of Scotland, Norway, north Sweden, Iceland, Greenland, north Asia and northern North America, and lives above the tree belt. Like the willow grouse it has three annual plumages. It feeds mostly on leaves and buds of birch, dwarf willow and heath plants as well as berries. Ptarmigan are monogamous and the male vigorously defends the incubating hen.

White-tailed Ptarmigan, *Lagopus leucurus,* 12 in. Found in mountain regions of western America from Alaska to New Mexico.

The *true pheasants,* Phasianinae, consist of some 150 species. In many the plumage of the males is so striking that they may be compared in beauty with the birds of paradise and the humming-birds. The group contains the partridges, quail and jungle-fowl in addition to the pheasants.

Barbary Partridge, *Alectoris barbara,* 13 in. Breeds in the mountain regions of Sardinia, Gibraltar and north Africa.

Rock Partridge, *Alectoris graeca,* 13½ in. Breeds in Italy, the Balkans and in Asia to China; it occurs in many different races.

Partridge, *Perdix perdix,* 12 in. Breeds everywhere in Europe, except in the northernmost and southernmost regions, as well as in large parts of Asia. It lives in dunes, heaths and cultivated ground, and feeds on weed seeds, corn, grass, clover, berries, worms and insects. The

(from above) Greater Prairie Chicken; Sage Grouse; Red Grouse; Willow Grouse; Ptarmigan; White-tailed Ptarmigan, winter and summer plumage

nest is a saucer-shaped hollow in the ground lined with straw. They lay 10-20 eggs which the female incubates alone; the male helps to look after the chicks, which are able to fly when they are about 10 days old.

Black Partridge, *Francolinus francolinus,* 13 in. Found in Cyprus, Asia Minor and eastwards to north India. Much hunted and now reduced in numbers.

Yellow-necked Spurfowl, *Pternistes leucoscopus,* 15 in. Common in dry areas of north-east Africa.

Crested Francolin, *Francolinus sephaena,* 10¼ in. Common around the upper Nile.

Himalayan Snowcock, *Tetraogallus himalayensis,* 27 in. Found in the Himalayas at heights above 12,000 ft.

Quail, *Coturnix coturnix,* 7 in. Breeds everywhere in Europe, except in the northernmost regions, as well as in Africa and large parts of Asia. The quail is the only truly migratory gallinaceous bird, for the European and

(from left, then from above) Barbary Partridge; Rock Partridge; Partridge; Black Partridge; Yellow-necked Spurfowl; Crested Francolin; Himalayan Snowcock; Quail; Painted Quail

(from above) Blood Pheasant; Impeyan Pheasant; Crimson Horned Pheasant; Cabot's Tragopan; Crested Wood Partridge

Asiatic individuals winter in Africa. It lives in corn and clover fields and seldom flies. The food consists of weed seeds and insects.

Painted Quail, *Excalfactoria chinensis,* 5 in. Found distributed from India through south-east Asia to Australia, mainly on steppe land.

Blood Pheasant, *Ithaginis cruentus,* 16-19 in., from central Asia. Is found in the mountain forests of the Himalayas and further east, at heights of 12,000-15,000 ft.

Impeyan Pheasant, *Lophophorus impejanus,* 27 in. Found in the Himalayas from Afghanistan to Bhutan, in summer up to the edge of the snow, in winter in the mountain forests.

Crimson Horned Pheasant, *Tragopan satyra,* 23 in. Found in Nepal and Bhutan, in dense mountain forests up to the snow line.

Cabot's Tragopan, *Tragopan caboti,* 23 in. Found in south-east China.

Crested Wood Partridge, *Rollulus roulroul,* 11 in. Found in south-east Asia. It goes about in pairs and feeds on insects, larvae, worms, berries, seeds and buds.

Common Pheasant, *Phasianus colchicus,* 21-35 in. Originates in the Caucasus, with over 30 races throughout Asia, and now introduced in most of Europe, North America and New Zealand. It lives in cultivated fields and on the edges of woods and spends the night up in the trees. The food consists mostly of weed seeds, corn, insects and larvae.

Pallas's Eared Pheasant, *Crossoptilon auritum,* 34 in. Found in east Tibet and west China, in the mountain forests up to heights of 12,000 ft. It is shy and can run fast, but seldom flies.

(left, from above) Common Pheasant; Chinese Silver Pheasant; Amherst Pheasant;
Golden Pheasant; Cheer Pheasant; *(right, from above)* Pallas's Eared Pheasant;
Koklas Pheasant; Bornean Fire-backed Pheasant; *(to right)* Reeves' Pheasant

(above) Jungle Fowl, male and female
(centre) Sonnerat's Jungle Fowl
(below) Javan Jungle Fowl

west China, at heights of 9,000-18,000 ft., where it feeds largely on bamboo shoots. It was introduced into Europe by Lady Amherst in 1828.

Koklas Pheasant, *Pucrasia macrolopha,* 21-25 in. Found in the Himalayas and south-west China.

Bornean Fire-backed Pheasant, *Lophura ignata,* 25 in. Found only in Borneo and is very rare.

Golden Pheasant, *Chrysolophus pictus,* 25 in. Found in mountain forests of central China. During the courtship dance the male holds out his collar, spreads his wings and raises his tail.

Cheer Pheasant, *Catreus wallichi,* 40 in. Found up to 6,000-12,000 ft. in the Himalayas, in rugged cliffs and scree country with sparse vegetation. It feeds on roots, bulbs and larvae.

Reeves' Pheasant, *Syrmaticus reevesi,* 82 in. Found in the mountain forests of north and west China. It feeds on acorns, chestnuts, berries, worms and insects.

Jungle Fowl, *Gallus gallus,* 17-27 in. Found in India, south-east Asia and Indonesia, in thick rain forests, particularly bamboo scrub. This is the original form from which domestic fowls have been developed.

Sonnerat's Jungle Fowl, *Gallus sonnerati,* 17-27 in. Found in west and south India. Some of the tail feathers of the male are much used in making salmon flies.

Javan Jungle Fowl, *Gallus varius,* 16-27 in. Found in Java and neighbouring islands. It lives along the coasts and in scrub valleys.

Common Peafowl, *Pavo cristatus,* 38-48 in., but up to 90 in. in the male

Chinese Silver Pheasant, *Gennaeus nycthemerus,* 35 in. Found in south China and Tonkin, and often kept in captivity both in its home country and elsewhere.

Amherst Pheasant, *Chrysolophus amherstiae,* 40-55 in. Found in south-eastern Tibet, north Burma and south-

with fully developed train. Found in India and Ceylon and now introduced as a park bird into many countries. It lives in clearings in the woods, often in large flocks. During courtship the male raises the train (upper tail coverts) and displays the brilliant colours and pattern.

Green Peafowl, *Pavo muticus,* 48-52 in. Found in south-east Asia and Java, and very common in forests along the rivers.

Congo Peacock, *Afropavo congensis,* 24-27 in. First found in 1936 in the Ituri Forest in the Congo.

Peacock Pheasant, *Polyplectron bicalcaratum,* 15-19 in. Found in the damp mountain forests of south-east Asia.

Argus Pheasant, *Argusianus argus,* 30-75 in. Found in the dense forests of Malaya and Sumatra. During courtship the male clears a place of grass, leaves and twigs, raises the long tail feathers and forms a pair of large fans with the broad wing feathers, displaying the eye-like markings.

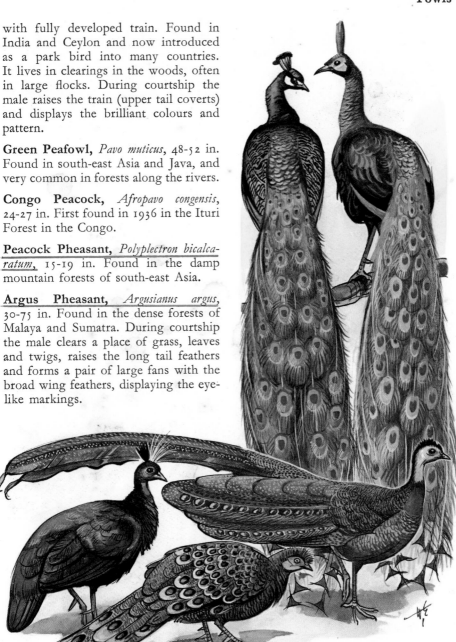

(above) Common Peafowl; Green Peafowl
(below) Congo Peacock; Peacock Pheasant; Argus Pheasant

Tinamous

(above) Bobwhite
(below) Gambel's Quail

The *American quails*, Odontophorinae, have a short thick beak with tooth-like serrations on the edge of the lower mandible, and lack spurs on the legs. They are all found in America, most in South America.

Bobwhite, *Colinus virginianus,* 8½ in. Found from south Canada through the United States to Mexico and Guatemala. It feeds in fields and open country and spends the night in bushes and low trees. The food consists of insects, berries and seeds. In the spring the males fight for the females, but they are monogamous. The female lays 12-24 eggs and the birds take turns to incubate.

Gambel's Quail, *Lophortyx gambeli,* 9 in. Found in desert areas of California, Arizona, New Mexico and Texas. Like other desert animals they can do without drinking water for long periods.

The TINAMOUS, Tinamiformes, is a small order with one family of fowl-like birds, which are active in the evening and at night, and are good runners but fly badly and have difficulty in steering. They are found from Mexico to southernmost South America, and feed on plant food and insects. The male, which is a little smaller than the female, scrapes a nest hollow and usually also incubates the bright glossy eggs and rears the young. The young leave the nest the day after hatching.

Spotted Tinamou, *Nothura maculosa,* 12 in. Found in the southern half of South America.

Rufous Tinamou, *Rhynchotus rufescens,* 15½ in. Found in Brazil, Paraguay, Uruguay and Argentina. The clutch consists of 5-9 eggs, but it is not certain whether it is the male or female which is responsible for incubation.

(above) Spotted Tinamou
(below) Rufous Tinamou

Kiwis

Kiwis, cassowaries, rheas and ostriches, were at one time all put into a single group. They are characteristically flightless running birds with a flat breast bone lacking a keel for the attachment of wing muscles, and with a much reduced wing skeleton. The feathers do not form a vane, but are divided up into threads and may be regarded as giant down. The distribution is largely in the warm regions of the southern hemisphere. It was at one time thought that these birds were all related; but there is no doubt that they originate from different groups of early birds and they are now classified in separate orders.

The kiwis, Apterygiformes, contain the true kiwis and the now extinct moas of New Zealand. These were large flightless birds, some larger than the African ostrich. The true kiwis consists of only three species, all found in the dense forests of New Zealand. They have a compact body, clothed with hair-like feathers, a long neck and a very long bill, and such small wings that no sign of them is visible externally; they are also tailless. The legs are powerful, the three front toes are relatively long with powerful digging claws and the back toe is short and has a powerful spur-like claw. In contrast to all other birds the kiwis have the nostrils right out on the tip of the beak. They are essentially nocturnal animals; they shelter by day in earth holes which they have dug themselves, often under the roots of a large tree. The food consists of worms and insects. The female is larger than the male and lays only one egg but it is 5 in. long.

Kiwis have been totally protected since 1921.

(above) Mantell's Kiwi; *(centre)* Kiwi, *(below)* Owen's Kiwi

Mantell's Kiwi, *Apteryx australis mantelli,* 20 in. A race of the common kiwi found in North Island, New Zealand. The plumage is harsh to the touch.

Kiwi, *Apteryx australis,* 20 in. Found principally in South Island and Stewart Island, New Zealand. The colouring is a lighter brown than in Mantell's kiwi and the plumage is soft to the touch.

Owen's Kiwi, *Apteryx oweni,* 19 in. Found in restricted areas of South Island, New Zealand.

(above) One-wattled Cassowary; Westermann's Cassowary; Bennett's Cassowary
(below) Common Cassowary; Emu

Cassowaries

THE CASSOWARY ORDER, Casuariiformes, contains two families, the true cassowaries and the emus, both found in the Australasian region.

True Cassowaries

The head has a large swollen casque, which helps to clear a way when the birds are going through undergrowth. The neck is naked and usually has one or more skin folds. The wing feathers lack a vane and the black shafts look rather like porcupine quills. The innermost of the three toes has a powerful slender claw, which is used as a weapon. Cassowaries can run at speeds of over 30 m.p.h., even through thick undergrowth, and they are particularly good swimmers. Their range is from New Guinea and the neighbouring islands to the northern coastal area of Australia. The food consists mostly of soft fruits. The female, which is significantly larger than the male, lays 3-6 eggs; the male is responsible for incubation and care of the young.

One-wattled Cassowary, *Casuarius unappendiculatus*, 54 in. Found in New Guinea and the islands to the west.

Bennett's Cassowary, *Casuarius bennetti*, 39 in. Found in New Guinea and New Britain, where it lives in mountain forests.

Westermann's Cassowary, *Casuarius bennetti papuanus*, 40 in. Found in north-west New Guinea.

Common Cassowary, *Casuarius casuarius*, 58 in. Found in western New Guinea, Ceram, the Aru Islands and northern Queensland, in several races.

Emus

The emu family, Dromiceidae, contains only one species; the others are extinct.

Emu, *Dromiceus novaehollandiae*, 76 in., and the second largest living bird. Found on the plains of eastern Australia and hunted because it competes for grazing with cattle and sheep; it also eats fruits. The reduced wings are hidden in the plumage. Emus run at speeds of 40 m.p.h. for short distances and swim well. They defend themselves by kicking backwards or to the side, unlike the cassowaries which kick forwards. The female lays 7-12 eggs, and the male takes care of incubation and rearing of the young.

Rheas

THE RHEAS, Rheiformes, live in South America and are the largest birds in this part of the world; they are also called American ostriches. The wings are proportionately long and have a claw at the

(from above) Common Rhea; Darwin's Rhea

tip which may be used as a weapon. The contour feathers lack barbules almost entirely. Rheas live on plant food, lizards, snails, worms and insects. They swim with almost the whole of the body submerged. The male, which is significantly larger than the female, collects a harem of 5-7 females which lay eggs in a nest he has scraped out; he alone incubates and rears the young.

Common Rhea, *Rhea americana*, 59 in. Found from north Brazil to south Argentina, essentially a steppe bird and a fast runner.

Darwin's Rhea, *Pterocnemia pennata*, 50 in. Found in the open country in Peru, Bolivia, Chile and Argentina.

Ostriches

THE OSTRICH ORDER, Struthioniformes, has only one species with several races, amongst others the Sahara ostrich, the Masai ostrich, the Somali ostrich and the Cape ostrich. The races may be distinguished by differences in the colour of the naked skin on the head and neck.

Ostrich, *Struthio camelus,* 79 in., and the largest living bird. The male is larger than the female and may weigh over 300 lb. It has only two toes, of which one is very large with a powerful hoof-like nail. Ostriches can run at speeds of 40 m.p.h., with a pace of up to 14 ft. They are found on the savannas of Africa from the Sahara southwards. They feed principally on fruits and other plant material, but also take small mammals, young birds, lizards and insects. The male usually collects 3-4 females and scrapes a hollow for the nest in which the females lay their eggs which weigh 3 lb; there are often 15-20 eggs in a nest. The male incubates by night and one of the females by day; sometimes the eggs are covered with sand and kept warm by the sun.

(from left) Somali Ostrich; Sahara Ostrich, female behind, male in front; Cape Ostrich

INDEX

Index

Index

Index

Index

NOTES